To
Sharon

A Great Ame...

Jack Jacobs

To Sharon
Sweet Anniv!
A
Gail

Mobocracy

From President Obama & Governor Walker
to the Occupy & Tea Party Movements
Mobocracy exposes the Cultural & Political
War to Destroy our Republic under God

Mobocracy

Jake Jacobs Ph. D.

LIFE SENTENCE Publishing

Mobocracy by Jake Jacobs Ph. D.

Copyright © 2012

PRINTED IN THE UNITED STATES OF AMERICA

LIFE SENTENCE Publishing and its logo are trademarks of LIFE SENTENCE Publishing, LLC

First edition published 2012

Library of Congress Control Number: 2012931164

LIFE SENTENCE Publishing, LLC

P.O. BOX 652

Abbotsford, WI 54405

www.lifesentencepublishing.com

ISBN: 978-1469904412

This book is available at Jake Jacobs' speaking engagements, www.jjusa.org, online, and at your local bookstore

This book is dedicated to the 2011 Governor of the Year, Scott Walker, who, as a Republican, defended our Republic under God during the chaos of mobocracy in Madison, Wisconsin, 2011–2012.

It is also dedicated to America's Founders who, with "reliance on the protection of divine providence," were willing for life and liberty to give of their lives, fortunes, and sacred honor for our republican form of government under God.

It is dedicated to my family: my wife Lori, whose faith in God and dedication to our family truly makes her a Proverbs 31 woman; my son Joseph, whose computer smarts have helped his old man figure out how to use a computer; and to my lovely daughter Anastasia, whose beautiful smile and kind heart always light up a room and bring us joy.

And last but not least is my dear friend Jo Leitner who, ironically, as a post-modern Lefty, encouraged me to write this book. He is one of the good ones!

ABOUT OUR COVER

John Adams' 1763 "An Essay on Man's Lust for Power" describes how democracy degenerates into anarchy or mobocracy. Our Founders did not give us a democracy but a glorious Constitutional Republic under God which is under heavy attack today on many cultural and political fronts across the United States. Throughout the streets and major institutions of America from Madison, Wisconsin to Oakland, California, New York City, Philadelphia, Atlanta, and L.A., there is an alarming and growing army of radical anti-republican anarchists, communists, socialists, unionists and a sundry of big government Left-wing ideologues who with fists held high cry out "this is what democracy looks like!"

European-socialist style mobs across America not only carry signs of the ubiquitous, militant, socialist-unionists' clenched fist, but their crowds are peppered with the flags and symbols of anarchists, communists, socialists, and unionists. As words like *democracy* and *republic* have meaning (see Chapter Three), so do flags, symbols, and signs, as they convey a worldview and philosophy. The atheist-communist choice of the classic red flag denotes their desire to eradicate free enterprise and our Republic under God from the earth. The anarchists black flag calls for revolutionary chaos in the streets as they defiantly demand no gods, no masters, and no authority. The classic anarchic-communist red and black flag in National Socialistic-style without the swastika represents the mob gone mad as they defy the rule of law in their naive attempt to usher in an earthly kingdom of social and economic justice through unjust means and violent measures. Unfortunately, many well-intentioned young adults, college students and respectable citizens have joined arm in arm with this cadre of anti-republic revolutionaries whose mobocratic machinations undermine freedom in America.

Wake up America, before it is too late! The mobocrats mean business. Study the mob, listen to their words, watch their ways and understand their demands to change and transform our Republic under God. Our Founders warned us that if we were to keep our Republic we would always have to remain diligent to the cause of freedom and vigilantly aware of those who would under the guise of freedom destroy life and liberty.

Semper Fi to the Republic!

Contents

INTRODUCTION

MADISON WISCONSIN'S WINTER WOODSTOCK

"A democracy is nothing more than mob rule, where
fifty-one percent of the people may take away the rights
of the other forty-nine."
*-Thomas Jefferson probably never said this
but he should have*

"A democracy is nothing more than mob rule, where
forty-nine percent of the people may take away the
rights of the other fifty-one as they tried to do in
Madison, Wisconsin, 2011–2012."
-Jake Jacobs, Wisconsin public school teacher

**A specter is haunting America
—the specter of democracy.**

After my interview defending Wisconsin Governor Scott
Walker with Fox & Friends during a bitterly cold Sunday
morning on February 20, 2011, I decided to walk around the
Capitol to observe and talk to many of the sign-carrying protestors.
What I saw that day and in my subsequent weekend visits to the
Capitol, throughout the mob's "Walker-Winter of Discontent,"
sent shivers down my spine and alarmed my heart, as it confirmed
our country's Founders' concerns over the "mob mindset" and
their defiance of the rule of law. Fourteen Democratic senators

left the state of Wisconsin and prevented a representative form of government—a republican form of government—from being used in Wisconsin, as their actions were a form of tyranny, or what James Madison called mobocracy, another word he used for democracy. The Democratic senators acted as mobocrats as they prevented the vote by the majority of senators who desired to represent their respective districts and the electoral majority in Wisconsin. The Democratic mobocrats violated their oath of office to support the U.S. Constitution, which guarantees a republican form of government.

As I heard the mob chant praise for the fourteen AWOL Democrats, I saw signs that called Governor Walker "Hitler," "Stalin," and "Mubarak"; signs that showed him hanging from a noose; signs that showed him in a gun sight that said "reload"; signs that made fun of his family and his education; and signs that asked why "Republicans hate people" and why "the Tea Party hates people." I saw anarchist, communist, socialist, and AFL-CIO signs all over the place. Workers World signs were peppered throughout the crowd advocating for teachers and students alike to join in the cause to end capitalism and advance communism. A very popular sign was the socialistworld.net sign calling for Wisconsin teachers to follow the teachings of Karl Marx to bring his worldview into the classroom and to emulate dictator Fidel Castro's right-hand man, the communist murderer Che Guevara.

And we wonder why so many high-schoolers and college kids adore Che and wear Che T-shirts and underwear.

There were signs attacking Israel and calling for a Palestinian state. There were signs for a greener earth and signs by La Raza calling for the southwestern part of the United States to become a part of "Greater Mexico," and signs defending illegal immigration. There were booths set up with left-wing paraphernalia, buttons showing Walker as a Nazi, books for sale on libertarian socialism, anarchy, progressive education, Obama, and Che Guevara, as well as copies of Karl Marx's *Communist Manifesto*, and Herbert Marcuse's works. At the end of the day I collected a large number of signs that were discarded to use as "artifacts" in my history classroom. Here are but a few examples of the thousands of various mob signs:

"Exterminating Union members"

"Governor Walker Makes Me Sick"

"Walker is a Turd! Madison Sewer Workers Local 236"

"Time to Stop the Imperial Walker!"

"Mubarak for Governor!"

"Wuck Falker"

"How many Tea Partiers Here Today are Wisconsin Voters?"

"Walker is a Wanker"

"Screw Us and We Multiply"

"Jesus was a Carpenter, Pontius Pilate was a Governor"

"Tea Baggers: Rich Man's Whores"

"Heil Walker! Stop The Maniac!"

"Hosni + Hitler = Dictator Scott Walker"

"Walker = Hitler, Repubs = Nazi Party, Wisconsin 2011= Germany"

1932, The New Jews = Public Employees-SIEG HEIL!"

"We took down Nixon, We'll take Down This Mother-f***er Too!"

"Hitler Hated Unions Too!"

"Fox News will lie about this"

Some signs were too vile and X-rated to include in the list. While I was not surprised to see hard-core union thugs holding violent and sophomoric signs, I was deeply concerned about seeing a large number of public school teachers carrying signs that not only reflected historical and political ignorance but that gave Governor Walker's budget the moral equivalency of Adolf Hitler's and Joseph Stalin's murderous governments. What I saw in Madison was a sad reflection of how radically left-wing many of Wisconsin's public school teachers are. And to think that they carry their twisted anti-American worldview into their classrooms. Those poor students in radical left-wing school districts like Madison and Milwaukee are being fed a daily dose of "politically correct" pabulum and lie after lie, as they were persuaded to call in "sick" and goose step with their mobocratic teachers.

Of the hodgepodge of protestors, the vast majority were Democrats and unionists, along with a significant number of anarchists, socialists, and communists. Jordan Petersen, a state-worker-turned-protest-organizer, explained to the CUNY teachers' union Clarion:

> There is something very special happening in this building. We've got anarchists and cops, socialists and small business owners, Green Party members and steel workers, teachers, and students, and dropouts all working together.

The mob happening was so special that Mary Bell, president of the teachers' union, the Wisconsin Education Association Council, four days earlier on Wednesday evening, February 16, had called for Wisconsin public school teachers to "drop out" of their jobs to come to Madison on Thursday and Friday to protest Republican plans to end collective bargaining for state employees. Bell claimed that she did not explicitly tell teachers to call in sick illegally; she was just suggesting that they "examine their hearts on where they should be." So many teachers called in sick on Thursday and Friday to illegally join Mary Bell's mob that school districts across the state were closed at taxpayers' expense. Some teachers were using bogus doctors' excuses, while a number of "blue flu" teachers were describing the protest as one big party, even playing the Beatles' song Revolution.

How apropos to have the mob playing socialist John Lennon's Revolution* song while "sick" teachers not only shut down schools across the state, but joined arm and arm in solidarity with their anarchist, socialist, communist, and unionist comrades to stop Republican legislation's attempt to balance the budget and to live within our financial means.

What many teachers didn't realize is that they were playing right into the hands of left-wing radicals whose agenda was to ignore the election results of November 2010 and the rule of law. Many well-intentioned teachers were being used as pawns in a much larger scheme to dismantle our republican form of government and replace it with mob rule, or democracy.

Winston Churchill could not have been more spot-on when he said, "The best argument against democracy is a five-minute conversation with the average voter." Many conversations I had with the average Wisconsin voter at the Capitol confirmed Churchill's dictum as it became apparent to me over and over again that our government-run schools, our university professors, and our elite media institutions have dumbed down many American citizens and, sadly, many public school teachers.

One lady, a middle school teacher, held a "Walker is Hitler" sign, and when asked why she equated Scott Walker to Adolf Hitler, she gave an incoherent explanation that, "Like Hitler, Walker is abolishing labor unions." And she is teaching our kids?! Thank you very much, WEAC, for protecting her right to be what Vladimir

---

*John Lennon's song Revolution has two versions, one of which advocates a Marxist revolution. See his January 21, 1971, Red Mole interview with Marxist Tariq Ali.

Lenin, the father of the Communist Russian revolution, called a "useful idiot." Unfortunately, there are far too many teachers like her in our government schools causing irreparable damage to Wisconsin's children!

I must qualify my indictment of many of the Radical-Left teachers I have encountered in Madison and in my career, especially at the many social studies conferences I attended throughout the years in Madison. I have worked with and know a number of dedicated, outstanding teachers who uphold traditional family values and do not accept the anti-American worldview as expressed by those in the Radical Left. Many of those teachers are afraid to speak out for fear of being ostracized, ridiculed, or intimidated by colleagues, union officials, and/or administrators. I know that while thousands of teachers called in "sick" throughout Wisconsin, not one that I know of did so where I worked. While a number of my colleagues no longer talked to me, said unkind things to me, or ripped up pictures of Governor Walker, they did not call in sick or join the mob in Madison. I wonder if that is due to certain Wisconsin school districts like mine being more conservative and still respecting the rule of law, while left-wing socialistic districts like Madison and Milwaukee believe in "mob rule" over state law and called for "sick-strikes" and for public school students to join in with the mob.

Eventually I found my way into the rotunda of Madison, Wisconsin's state Capital, to observe those who had illegally taken over "the people's house." The place stunk from days of use as a Winter Woodstock. The popular socialist fist sign was all over the place, a sign used by the AFL-CIO, the International Socialist Organization, and Students for a Democratic Society (SDS), the 1960s radical group that morphed into militant terrorists like Barack Obama's political teaching friends, professors Bill Ayers and Bernardine Dohrn.

Ugly makeshift signs were taped all over the Capitol's beautiful marble, and people were sleeping and camping throughout the building, with bizarre slogans, silly chants, goofy outfits, and incessant drum beating with naive ominous, Wagnerian, and Nurenbergian cries of:

"This is what democracy looks like!"

Anarchist, socialist, and Marxist websites expressed elation over the tens of thousands of mobocrats who gathered in Madison chanting over and over again, "This is what democracy looks like!"

The Marxist website *Workers' Liberty* for international working class solidarity and socialism put it this way:

> Last Saturday, over 100,000 people rallied in Madison in the largest demonstration Madison has seen in 40 years. The response by private sector unions has been excellent, with no apparent split between private and public sectors. The favorite chant was, "This is what democracy looks like!"—the slogan of the 1990s global justice movement.

The 1990s Global Justice Movement was a network of anarchists, Marxists, socialists, progressives, and a number of Radical

Leftists demanding an "equal" distribution of economic resources through state dictates. Sadly, this IS what democracy looks like— the mob using the state to confiscate the people's hard-earned money so it can be spent by Democratic politicians for political power and social programs that are ineffectual and perpetuate greed under the guise of need.

What I experienced in Madison, Wisconsin, during the Left's Winter Woodstock of 2011 confirmed what Founding Father James Madison, the fourth president of the United States, my Capital's namesake, had warned Americans about:

Themselves and the Mob.

CHAPTER 1

DEMOCRACY VERSUS A REPUBLIC UNDER GOD

"Between a balanced republic and a democracy, the
difference is like that between order and chaos."
-John Marshall

James Madison, the Father of the Constitution and a student of the nature of governments throughout the ages, was equally a student of human nature. He wrote in Federalist Paper No. 51:

> It may be a reflection on human nature, that such devices should be necessary to control the abuses of government. But what is government itself, but the greatest of all reflections on human nature? If men were angels, no government would be necessary. If angels were to govern men, neither external nor internal controls on government would be necessary. In framing a government which is to be administered by men over men, the great difficulty lies in this: you must first enable the government to control the governed; and in the next place oblige it to control itself.

This is why James Madison and America's Founders NEVER trusted democracy!

Knowing that men were not angels and in many cases were driven by greed, emotions, selfishness, insecurity, "group think," and the mob mentality, Madison and the fifty-five luminaries of the Constitutional Convention, in framing our type of government, rejected democracy and explicitly and specifically created in our rule book—the Constitution, in Article 4, Section 4, "a republican form of government." It reads in full:

> **Section 4.** The United States shall guarantee to every State in this Union a Republican Form of Government, and shall protect each of them against Invasion; and on Application of the Legislature, or of the Executive (when the Legislature cannot be convened) against domestic Violence.

Americans have grown accustomed to hearing and using the word democracy for our form of government. Professors will tell you it's purely semantics and not important to distinguish between the two.

I beg to differ.

It was vitally important to our Founders, when deliberating on what form of government to create, that they very explicitly and unabashedly did not call for a democracy but a republican form of government under God. Here are but a few of the hundreds of examples of our Founders' negative views on democracy:

"Between a balanced republic and a democracy, the difference is like that between order and chaos." —John Marshall

"Democracies have ever been spectacles of turbulence and contention; have ever been found incompatible with personal security, of the rights of property, and have in general, been short in their lives as they have been violent in their deaths." —James Madison

"A simple democracy...is one of the greatest evils." —Benjamin Rush

"Pure democracy cannot subsist long nor be carried far into the departments of state—it's very subject to caprice and the madness of popular rage." —John Witherspoon

"Remember, democracy never lasts long. It soon wastes, exhausts, and murders itself. There never was a democracy yet that did not commit suicide. It is in vain to say that democracy is less vain, less proud, less selfish, less ambitious, or less avaricious than aristocracy or monarchy. It is not true, in fact, and nowhere appears in history. Those passions are the same in all men, under all forms of simple government, and when unchecked, produce the same effects of fraud, violence, and cruelty." —John Adams

"The experience of all former ages had shown that of all human governments, democracy was the most unstable, fluctuating and short-lived." —John Quincy Adams

"A democracy is a volcano which conceals the fiery materials of its own destruction. These will produce an

eruption and carry desolation in their way. The known propensity of a democracy is to licentiousness which the ambitious call, and ignorant believe to be liberty."
—Fisher Aimes

"In democracy...there are commonly tumults and disorders...Therefore a pure democracy is generally a very bad government. It is often the most tyrannical government on earth." —Noah Webster

"A democracy is nothing more than mob rule, where fifty-one percent of the people may take away the rights of the other forty-nine percent." —Thomas Jefferson*

Historians Charles and Mary Beard confirmed our Founders views on democracy when in 1939 they wrote:

> At no time, at no place, in solemn convention assembled, through no chosen agents, had the American people officially proclaimed the United States to be a democracy. The Constitution did not contain the word or any word lending countenance to it... When the Constitution was framed, no respectable person called himself a democrat.

Describing democracy as evil, violent, unstable, cruel, licentious, fraudulent, mad, turbulent, and tyrannical, our Founders vehemently rejected democracy and wholeheartedly embraced a Republican form of government under God!

It is difficult for many Americans in our post-modern, anti-Judeo-Christian day and age to understand the difference between

---

*Historians debate whether Jefferson ever said this.

democracy and republicanism as understood in our Founders' pro-Judeo-Christian world of 1776.

A Republic under God is the KEY distinction.

According to our Founders, in a republic the people hold individual sovereign power and elect representatives who exercise that power. In contrast, in a pure democracy the people or community as an organized whole wield the sovereign power of government. This is why our Founders called the democratic collective whole of 51 percent potentially "mob rule." In a democracy, the individual is not sovereign; rather, the collective majority is sovereign. Remember that in 1776 our Founders were dealing with a "divine right of kings" monarchical-government concept that gave sovereignty to only one individual, the king! A democracy has no sovereign individuals, as individual citizens are at the mercy of the collective whole or potentially the mob. In a republic, ALL individuals hold sovereign power or are essentially kings with the divine right of life and liberty! That is why Thomas Jefferson, Benjamin Franklin, and John Adams, in the Declaration of Independence, acknowledge God—not the government or the democratic majority—as the source of individual sovereign rights of life and liberty. In a republican form of government under God, an individual's unalienable rights cannot be denied or violated by the democratic majority, or the mob madness of the minority, as experienced in Madison, Wisconsin, during early 2011. James Madison and our Founders understood that the central feature in a democracy is a collectivist political philosophy that denies

God-given and unalienable individual rights. That is why it was a natural fit for anarchists, socialists, communists, and secular progressives to join the minority mob, the teachers, and their unions in Madison, proclaiming, "This is what democracy looks like!" That IS what democracy looks like: a disgruntled minority or majority denying the individual rights and representative republican voice of the people of Wisconsin.

I love this definition of democracy that reflects our Founders' worldview and what was exercised in the Madison mob's "Walker is Hitler" protest:

> Democracy is a government of the masses where authority is derived through mass meeting or any other form of direct expression, resulting in Mobocracy. Their attitude toward property is communistic—negating property rights. Their attitude toward law is anti-Constitutional in that the will of the majority shall regulate, whether it be based upon deliberation or governed by passion. They are prejudiced and impulsive without restraint or regard to consequences, resulting in demagoguism, license, agitation, discontent, and anarchy.

We are living in a day and age that reflects the prophetic voice of Founder Benjamin Franklin who feared our republic's death as we regressed into a democracy. Franklin warned:

> When the people find that they can vote themselves money, that will herald the end of the republic.

From the mobocrats in Madison to the "Eat the Rich" Occupy mobocrat movement across America, there is an ever-growing "give-me, give-me" mob mindset that demands other people's money with no consideration of their individual God-given right to keep their property. If not checked, this mob madness will lead to the eventual death of our Republic under God.

This is why as a free citizen of America and Wisconsin I opposed the confiscation of my money by the National Education Association and the Wisconsin Education Association Council.

During one of my return visits to Madison in that mad winter of 2011 to defend Governor Walker, I was swarmed by tens of thousands of mobocrats who kept shouting over and over again, "This IS what democracy looks like!!" "Kill the bill!" and "Stop Union busting!" This Madison mob was demanding more money through WEAC coercion from the taxpayers who had inherited Democratic Governor Doyle's deficit budget of $3.6 billion.

When I and one brave citizen carrying an "I support Walker" sign began counter-shouting, "Free to Choose!" a protestor in the crowd asked me, "Why are you chanting, 'Free to choose'?" I explained that as a free citizen I should not have my money, my property, confiscated by the NEA-WEAC for ideas, politics, and policies I disagree with, and that a citizen should never be put into a position of conflicting interests as a government employee and a taxpayer. That is why both FDR and Jimmy Carter, while defending private unions, signed legislation against federal public unions, knowing that they create a profound conflict of interest that is unjust and immoral. It was Thomas Jefferson who said, "To compel a man to furnish funds for the propagation of ideas he disbelieves and abhors is sinful and tyrannical." Later on, one mobocrat hit me with his sign and threatened to shove his boot up my derriere. I retorted: "You just proved my point."

Whether it is unjust and immoral or sinful and tyrannical, the NEA-WEAC has not only confiscated millions of dollars from unsuspecting or suspecting teachers, but they have a democratic or mobocratic agenda that threatens the very survival of our Republic under God. I will cover more on the corrupt NEA in chapter thirteen.

Now it may be asked: "Did not the followers of Thomas Jefferson use the term 'democratic republic'?"

Yes, they did, and while it is true that the term was used, the ultimate and final form was a "republican form of government" utilizing the "democratic process." The democratic process functions within a republican form of government, meaning that the people do have a say and participate in their government but with delineations and limitations.

Theoretically, a democracy involves full participation of all the people in the legislative processes of government. This has never worked throughout history because "the people," in their busy lives, have neither the time nor the inclination to study and know the issues. Coupled with the propensity for individuals to only participate in politics for selfish interests and not for the common good, various expressions of democracy have failed miserably and led to tyranny, as seen in the Greek city-states. The Greek philosopher Aristotle tells us in his book, *Politics*, "that man is by nature a political animal," and if not checked by the temperance of his ways, will reap a society where "everyone lives as he wants and towards whatever end he happens to crave."

This principle would apply to the manipulated masses as well as to the dictator, the tyrant, and the oligarchs who control and rule with money and power. Like Thomas Jefferson, Aristotle realized that 51 percent, or the majority, of the people could be as foolish, selfish, and tyrannical as any oligarch or dictator.

Aristotle called democracy a perversion.

Like Aristotle, the Founding Fathers had good reason to think of democracy with derision. They knew the history of democracy in the early Greek city-states, a democracy which produced some of the wildest excesses of big-brother government imaginable, leading in every case to mob rule, then anarchy, and finally tyranny under an oligarchy. During that period in Greece, there was a lawyer named Solon who urged the creation of a fixed body of laws, which were not to be subject to majority whims and mob demands. Unfortunately, the Greeks never adopted his ideas.

The Romans adopted Solon's ideas and created the twelve tables of the Roman law and built a republic that limited government control over the people and left the people alone. Since government was limited, the people were free to pursue life and to create and produce, with the understanding that they could keep the fruits of their labor. Eventually Rome became wealthy, a master of innovative ideas, and the envy of the world.

The great Roman philosopher Cicero, whom our Founders were fond of admiring and quoting, purposely translated the Greek word *politeia* (polity or politics) with the Latin word *res publica*, knowing that the words *demos* (people) and *kratos* (power), giving us *demokratia* or democracy, is "people power," and that "people power" could easily distort the ability and opportunity for the people to live in a free society.

As a population grows and governing becomes more distant to the people, or the people become more distant to the government, democracy becomes more and more inefficient, contentious, and turbulent.

To reiterate what James Madison wrote in Federalist Paper No. 10:

> Democracies have ever been spectacles of turbulence and contention; have ever been found incompatible with personal security or the rights of property; and have in general been as short in their lives as they have been violent in their deaths... a republic, by which I mean a government in which the scheme of representation takes place, opens a different prospect and promises the cure for which we are seeking.

Madison goes on to explain that as a country expands, it cannot accommodate the people within the limitations of a democracy, but must utilize the much more effective representative or republican form of government to protect the growing interests and issues of the people. Once again, here is Madison in Federalist Paper No. 10:

> In a democracy the people meet and exercise the government in person; in a republic they assemble and administer it by their representatives and agents. A democracy, consequently, must be confined to a small spot. A republic may be extended over a large section.

Democracies work fine if we're talking about a family deciding where to go on vacation or what to have for supper, but when you realize how much work is involved in having millions and millions of people in a country as large as the United States vote on every single issue brought up in Congress every day, common sense tells us why our Founding Fathers gave us a republican form of government and not a democracy.

Our Founders knew this well because, as stated earlier, all attempts at democracy in early Greek history failed and actually produced some of the most tyrannical governments in the history of the world.

This is why James Madison in Federalist Paper No. 10 says: "A republic, by which I mean a government in which the scheme of representation takes place, opens a different prospect and promises the cure for which we are seeking." Our Founders pointed out that as the United States expands, democracy would prove ineffectual as it always had in history and could only work on a limited basis within a confined small area.

James Madison once again stresses republicanism in Federalist Paper No. 39, explaining in no uncertain terms what a republic is:

> We may define a republic to be... a government which derives all its powers directly or indirectly from the great body of the people, and is administered by persons holding their offices during pleasure for a limited period, or during good behavior. It is essential to such a government that it be derived from the great body of society, not from an inconsiderable proportion of a favored class of it; otherwise a handful of tyrannical nobles, exercising their oppressions by a delegation of their powers, might aspire to the rank of republicans and claim for their government the honorable title of republic.

Why did James Madison stress that our republic's representatives hold their offices during "good behavior?" That will be the topic of our next chapter.

Jake Jacobs in Madison with Mob Souvenirs

Used with permission — visit ConservativeDailyNews.com

CHAPTER 2

GOD'S LAW & GOOD BEHAVIOR IS ESSENTIAL TO A REPUBLIC

"Our constitution was made only for a moral and religious people. It is wholly inadequate to the government of any other."
-John Adams

"God's law is 'right reason'. When perfectly understood it is called 'wisdom'. When applied by government in regulating human relations it is called 'justice'."
-Marcus Tullius Cicero

"Good behavior" is why our Founders emphasized establishing a republican form of government under God. By now you've noticed my emphasis on a **republican form of government under God.** The reason I emphasize it is quite simple.

Our Founders did.

When I write letters to the editor, write my blog articles, and give speeches across America, I emphasize our **Republic under God**, and there is always one person in the crowd or audience who protests to me that America is not a Republic under God, but a secular, humanistic democracy free from God.

Nothing could be further from the truth!

This FACT needs to be clearly understood today as our Founders understood it. One of the major flaws or weaknesses in a democracy is that it is far too often driven by majority feelings that demand nothing less than what they believe they deserve from the minority. Or in the case of the mob in Madison, Wisconsin, during their 2011 winter of discontent, it was a minority who, while rejecting the election results of 2010, demanded nothing less than what they believe they deserve from the majority.

During my visit to the Capitol in Madison, Wisconsin, to observe and talk with the Occupy crowd, one sign read, "Don't accept less than you deserve 99%!" When I asked the sign owner, a student at the University of Wisconsin-Madison, the meaning of her sign, she said, "We the people, the 99%, demand from the rich 1% of what is owed us!" When I asked her why it was owed to her, she rambled on about social injustice, inequality, racism, fascism, sexism, and a myriad of other disjointed and discombobulated ideas sewn together with her feelings, as expressed, she said, by the masses of the people, the so-called 99%.

This young lady is a classic example of "This is what democracy looks like," sounds like, thinks like, acts like, and feels like and why our Founders warned us to avoid democracy like the plague!

This is why our Founders often called democracy, the mob!

Democracy's source of law is the arbitrary and flighty feelings of the masses, the mob that demands stealing from the producers—the real workers in society—and distributing the stolen goods to the masses. The mobocrats' immature behavior, naive assumptions, and ignorant mindset make a mockery of our constitutional Republic under God.

But even in a republic one has the freedom to be foolish.

Our Founders wisely rejected mob feelings as the source of law because that law would be unreliable and unstable. The mob majority in a democracy could vote to make murder legal, or redistribution of wealth legal, or abortion legal, thus violating many of the laws given to mankind by God Almighty.

The foundation of America's law and for America's lawmakers and citizens was, according to our Founders, God's Law, His Torah, His teachings for mankind from the Holy Scriptures.

Founder Noah Webster states it succinctly when he writes: "Our citizens should early understand that the genuine source of correct republican principles is the Bible, particularly the New Testament, or the Christian religion."

In a democracy, mores and values are dictated by feelings of convenience, libertinism, and wants that can easily change with the wind, with dissatisfaction with election results, or with the majority vote. Mob principles are always in flux with no absolute foundation to anchor upon. In the relativistic world of fluctuating, emotional, democratic feelings that are almost always self-serving, selfish, whimsical, and controlling, there is a rejection of universal, eternal principles that applies to all citizens at all times. Founding Father Benjamin Rush observed: "Where there is no law, there is no liberty; and nothing deserves the name of law but that which is certain and universal in its operation upon all the members of the community."

In our American Republic under God, His principles are universal, constant, certain, and unchanging, reflecting His perfect character, justice, and love.

It is imperative for Americans to grasp why America's Founders believed that the key to a successful republic was for it to be structured on the foundation of God's law as revealed in the Bible. Our Founders, as students of government in history, knew that almost all governments were corrupt because man was sinful and corrupt.

This foundational "Genesis reality" of human nature is clearly laid out in the Judeo-Christian worldview as explained in the Scriptures. From the teachings of Moses and the Hebrew prophets, to Jesus the Messiah and the Apostles came the development of the university where students would discover the wonder of God's universe. In the Judeo-Christian worldview, the universe or "uni-verse" (uni = single and verse = sentence) or "single spoken sentence" was created by the LORD God in a single spoken sentence. A "university" Christian education from Oxford and Cambridge or Harvard and Yale presupposed that "In the beginning God created the heavens and the earth," and along with that presupposition came the belief that God's laws were an integral component of mankind's relationship to each other and to God. One of the most widely read and influential authorities on the subject of law and America's Founders was the Englishman Professor William Blackstone.

Blackstone taught law at Oxford, and his popular lectures as well as his *Commentaries on the Laws of England* were widely read in America. Introduced in 1766, Blackstone's *Commentaries* became *the* primary law book of the Founding Fathers.

Blackstone taught, "When the Supreme Being formed the universe... he impressed certain principles upon that matter, from which it can never depart, and without which it would cease to be." When speaking of murder, Blackstone states in his *Commentaries*: "To instance in the case of murder: this is expressly forbidden by the divine... If any human law should allow or enjoin to commit it, we are bound to transgress that human law..."

Here is how Blackstone explains the laws of nature:

> Man, considered as a creature, must necessarily be subject to the laws of his Creator, for he is entirely a dependent being... And consequently, as man depends absolutely upon his Maker for everything, it is necessary that he should in all points conform to his Maker's will. This will of his Maker is called the law of nature.

> This law of nature, being coeval (coexistent) with mankind and dictated by God Himself, is of course superior in obligation to any other. It is binding over all the globe, in all countries, and at all times; no human laws are of any validity, if contrary to this.

According to Blackstone, the laws of nature are the will of God for man. He continues:

> And if our reason were always... clear and perfect... the task would be pleasant and easy; we should need no

other guide but (the law of nature). But every man now finds the contrary in his own experience; that his reason is corrupt, and his understanding full of ignorance and error. This has given manifold occasion for the benign interposition of Divine Providence; which... hath been pleased, at sundry times and in diverse manners, to discover and enforce its laws by an immediate and direct revelation. The doctrines thus delivered we call the revealed or divine law, and they are to be found only in the Holy Scriptures.

Blackstone's phrase, "the law of nature's God," is the revealed or divine law, God's law, found in the Holy Scriptures. Blackstone's conclusion couples these two phrases:

"Upon these two foundations, the law of nature and the law of revelation (the law of nature's God), depend all the human laws; that is to say, no human laws should be suffered to contradict these."

As mentioned earlier, our Founders had a deep appreciation for the wisdom of great thinkers of antiquity, and one of their favorite philosophers outside of Moses and Jesus was Cicero. Marcus Tullius Cicero, a contemporary of Julius Caesar, studied philosophy in Athens and law in Rome. He became one of the supreme lawyers of his day and was a member of the Roman consul. In his classic works, *On the Republic* and *On the Laws*, he concluded that the most effective and successful form of government was a republic based on natural law or God's law. Professor William

Ebenstein of Princeton, in his book, *Great Political Thinkers*, has this to say about Cicero's view on "true law":

> True law is right reason in agreement with nature; it is of universal application, unchanging and everlasting; it summons to duty by its commands, and averts from wrongdoing by its prohibitions... It is a sin to try to alter this law, nor is it allowable to repeal any part of it, and it is impossible to abolish entirely. We cannot be freed from its obligations by senate or people, and we need not look outside ourselves for an expounder or interpreter of it. And there will not be different laws at Rome and Athens, or different laws now and in the future, but one eternal and unchangeable law will be valid for all nations and all times, and there will be one master and ruler, that is God, over us all, for he is the author of this law, its promulgator, and its enforcing judge. Whoever is disobedient is fleeing from himself and denying his human nature, and by reason of this very fact he will suffer the worst punishment.

Professor Edward Clayton reflects on Cicero's ideas behind a successful republican form of government:

> As has been said, Cicero subordinated philosophy to politics, so it should not surprise us to discover that his philosophy had a political purpose: the defense, and if possible the improvement, of the Roman Republic. The politicians of his time, he believed, were corrupt and no longer possessed the virtuous character that had been the main attribute of Romans in the earlier days of Roman history. This loss of virtue was, he believed, the cause

of the Republic's difficulties. He hoped that the leaders of Rome, especially in the Senate, would listen to his pleas to renew the Republic. This could only happen if the Roman elite chose to improve their characters and place commitments to individual virtue and social stability ahead of their desires for fame, wealth, and power. Having done this, the elite would enact legislation that would force others to adhere to similar standards, and the Republic would flourish once again.

While Cicero lived fifty years before Jesus Christ, you'd think he was talking about Washington, D.C. or Madison, Wisconsin, in the twenty-first century. Like America's Founders, he understood human nature and the propensity for politicians to be corrupt and lacking in virtue. Cicero equated the success of a republic with upright character and individual virtue that relied on God's universal law for guidance.

In our Founders' historical, philosophical, and political studies, they discovered a familiar theme that ran through the minds and works of Greco-Roman and Judeo-Christian philosophers such as Aristotle, Demosthenes, Salon, Seneca, and especially Cicero, as well as many of the European, English, and Scottish Christian political philosophers such as Samuel Rutherford, Edward Coke, John Locke, Montesquieu, and William Blackstone. That familiar theme was that "true law" was ultimately natural law or God's law, which was "one eternal, unchangeable law valid for all nations at all times."

It is no wonder that Thomas Jefferson and the Committee of Five, when drafting the Declaration of Independence, utilized the commonly used and commonly understood Greco-Roman, Judeo-Christian phrase "the laws of nature and nature's God." In the first paragraph of the Declaration of Independence it reads:

> When in the course of human events it becomes necessary for one people to dissolve the political bands which have connected them with another and to assume among the powers of the earth the separate and equal station to which the laws of nature and of nature's God entitles them, a decent respect to the opinions of mankind requires that they should declare the causes which impel them to the separation.

The violation of "the laws of nature and nature's God" by Great Britain was the reason the Founders declared independence from their tyranny, arguing that they were entitled to establish themselves among the powers of the earth as a separate and equal station. Sadly, we have lost the biblical concept of "the laws of nature and of nature's God," as those eight words seem to carry no special significance for most Americans, and are especially ignored or ridiculed by the mobocrats and the Radical Left in America.

In our Founders' day, that eight-word phrase described a complete philosophy of life and a biblical worldview that is rejected by the practitioners of democracy and widely ignored in our secular, post-modern universities today. It is no coincidence that the symbol of the mobocrat anarchists that was quite common at the Occupy and Madison "Walker is Hitler" rallies is the 'circle

A' with the words "no gods, no masters, against all authority," or that the mobocrat socialists and communists love to quote Karl Marx's dictum, "The idea of God is the keynote of a perverted civilization. It must be destroyed!" The mindset of the mobocrat lacks a proper understanding of our Founders' Judeo-Christian worldview. The "laws of nature" to them is doing what comes naturally or, to paraphrase the words of seventeenth-century Christian philosopher John Locke, "man in a state of nature without the Divine Law will create a state of chaos." They reject outright the moral ramification of "nature's God" and that the source of our rights is our Creator who is called in the Declaration of Independence "the Supreme Judge of the world."

The Founders reflect the same biblical worldview and values in Blackstone's *Commentaries*, for example, when James Wilson, signer of the Constitution and a Supreme Court member, states:

> All laws, however, may be arranged in two different classes. 1) Divine. 2) Human... But it should always be remembered that this law, natural or revealed, made for men or for nations, flows from the same Divine source: it is the law of God... Human law must rest its authority ultimately upon the authority of that law which is Divine.

Alexander Hamilton writes:

> "The law... dictated by God Himself is, of course, superior in obligation to any other. It is binding over all the globe, in all countries, and at all times. No human laws are of any validity if contrary to this."

This is reiterated by Rufus King, another signer of the Constitution, when he writes:

> The law established by the Creator extends over the whole globe, is everywhere and at all times binding upon mankind... This law of God by which he makes his way known to man and is paramount to all human control.

There are hundreds of such writings by our Founders who recognized the absolute necessity of God's law in an intimate, inextricable relationship with a successful republican form of government. When our Founders sought to build "one nation under God," they purposely established their legal codes on the foundation of natural law or God's law. They believed that our republic should be governed, as Thomas Jefferson put it:

> By the moral law to which man has been subjected by his Creator, and of which his feelings, or conscience as it is sometimes called, are the evidence with which his Creator has furnished him. The moral duties which exist between individuals in a state of nature accompany them into a state of society,... their Maker not having released them from those duties on their forming themselves into a nation.

From the inception of our constitutional republican form of government, God's law was the guiding legal principle in the land by not only our presidents and Congress, but also by the Supreme Court.

Earl Taylor, director of the National Center for Constitutional Studies, writes:

> In the view of the Court, its members were to decide cases by exercising "that understanding which Providence has bestowed upon them" (Gibbons v. Ogden, 22 U.S. 1, 186-87, 1824). Since the laws they adjudicated were based on "the preexisting and higher authority of the laws of nature" (The West River Bridge Company v. Joseph Dix, 47 U.S. 507, 532, 1848), they relied less on judicial precedent than on "eternal justice as it comes from intelligence... to guide the conscience of the Court" (Rhode Island v. Massachusetts, 39 U.S. 210, 225, 1840).

> In the 1900s, however, the Court began to depart from the original American philosophy. By 1947, Justice Hugo Black (following the earlier reasoning of Justice Oliver Wendell Holmes) was urging that "the 'natural law' formula... should be abandoned;" he even argued that it was "a violation of our Constitution!" (Adamson v. California, 332 U.S. 46, 75, 1947). The other branches of the federal government have also succumbed to this new line of thinking.

> Today, the United States has all but severed its connection to "the laws of nature and of nature's God." We've sold our birthright for a "mess of pottage," and we now find ourselves harvesting the fruits of that decision. In the recent words of Fifth Circuit Court of Appeals Judge Edith H. Jones, our country has plunged into a profound moral crisis "because we have lost the sense of a God who takes interest in what we do." As a result,

she says, we have come to tolerate violence, immorality, and the disintegration of our families, and "are only now beginning to reap the whirlwind consequences" of these evils. We are reminded of this sober admonition from the Old Testament prophet Hosea:

Hear the word of the Lord, ye children of Israel: for the Lord hath a controversy with the inhabitants of the land, because there is no truth, nor mercy, nor knowledge of God in the land... My people are destroyed for lack of knowledge: because thou hast rejected knowledge, I will also reject thee,... seeing thou hast forgotten the law of thy God, I will also forget thy children.

Not only have Americans and our politicians forgotten "the law of God," but they rarely if ever are taught the proper principles of our Republic under God. They do not realize that the word democracy never appears in our Constitution; our Constitution says we are to have a "republican form of government" and, as earlier stated, our Founders very implicitly rejected the word democracy to describe our form of government. How is it that famous Americans from both political parties today, and in our recent history, have used the word democracy in place of republic or interchanged them as synonyms in their dialogues?

The answer is much more nefarious than our professors would have us believe. Many of our teachers for years have said, "Oh, it's no big deal; it's only semantics; they have the same meanings."

No they don't and the following chapter will explain why.

CHAPTER 3

WORDS HAVE MEANING

"When I use a word it means just what I choose it to
mean—neither more nor less."
-Humpty Dumpty

Words do have meanings that convey ideas and, as we all know, ideas have consequences. As I have expressed earlier, our wise Founders very carefully, deliberately, and painstakingly chose specific and particular words when crafting our Constitution to assure Americans of the most effective form of government that would preserve in perpetuity their God-given rights of life and liberty.

Why is it, then, that the brilliant and only Ph.D. president, Democrat Woodrow Wilson, would claim that World War I was the "war to make the world safe for democracy?" Or that the equally savvy Democratic President Franklin Roosevelt would declare during World War II that America would be "the great arsenal of Democracy"?

Due to the serious nature of creating a "new" government, and to avoid misinformation, the Constitutional Convention of 1787 was held in strict secrecy. When the convention was over, excited citizens gathered outside Independence Hall to discover what form of government our Founders had designed. As Benjamin Franklin left the convention hall, a Mrs. Powel of Philadelphia asked Benjamin Franklin, "Well, Doctor, what have we got, a republic or a monarchy?" Without hesitation, Franklin responded, "A republic, if you can keep it."

James McHenry, signer of the Constitution and president of the Maryland Bible Society (Madison, Wisconsin's Henry Street is named after him), recorded this exchange in a diary entry that was later reproduced in the 1906 American Historical Review. Unfortunately, Franklin's "republic" response has been misquoted far too many times as having been,

"A democracy, if you can keep it."

Even the NRA's conservative Republican Charlton Heston quoted Franklin this way, for example, in a CBS 60 Minutes interview with Mike Wallace that was aired on December 20, 1998. Heston is not the only one.

Here are but a few of the thousands of examples of the use of the word democracy by both political parties when they should be saying republic or republicanism:

"Democracy is... the only path to national success and dignity." —Republican President George W. Bush

"We must revitalize our democracy." —Democratic President Bill Clinton

"The practice of listening to opposing views is essential for effective citizenship. It is essential for our democracy." —Democratic President Barack Obama

Even my hero, Republican President Ronald Reagan, whom I meet in 1998 in his L.A. office, as one of the last Americans to do so, passionately stated:

"Democracy is worth dying for, because it's the most deeply honorable form of government."

O' President Reagan, whom I miss so much, "Democracy is not worth dying for," and it is not a "deeply honorable form of government," for in it lies the mob, tyranny, and the death of freedom.

However, if properly understood, our Republic under God is worth dying for, for in IT freedom flourishes and liberty and life prosper!

I could list hundreds of more examples of the misuse of the word democracy for our form of government. Let it suffice to say that the American mindset has drifted far from our Founders' original intent for the words used and the republican form of government they wonderfully designed in 1787.

We've all heard the word democracy used in place of republic countless times by our teachers, journalists, reporters, politicians, and presidents. Democracy and republic are unfortunately used interchangeably in modern political discourse, yet as we have explained, their true original meanings are very different. George Orwell wrote about "meaningless words" that are endlessly repeated in the political arena. Orwell explained that words like democracy and republic have been abused and misused for so long that their original meanings have been distorted and misapplied. In Orwell's view, many political words were "often used in a consciously dishonest way." Without precise meanings behind words, politicians and elites can obscure reality and condition people to reflexively associate certain words with positive or negative perceptions. In other words, unpleasant facts can be hidden behind purposely meaningless language. As a result, Americans have been conditioned to accept the word democracy as a synonym for republic and freedom, and have been led to believe that democracy is unquestionably good. Ironically, a classic example of the perversion of words is illustrated in the official names of the three "evil empires": the USSR, PRC, and DPRK, or Union of Soviet Socialist Republics, the People's Republic of China, and the Democratic People's Republic of Korea, respectively. A true republic is a vanguard of life and liberty, not death and destruction as practiced by Communist Russia and North Korea, and Marxist China.

As we have explained, from Aristotle to Cicero, to James Madison and Thomas Jefferson, democracy is not freedom. Democracy is simply majoritarianism, which is inherently incompatible with real liberty. That is why the father of the Russian-Communist-Socialist Revolution, Vladimir Lenin, called his followers within the Russian Social Democratic Labor Party (RSDLP) the Bolsheviks, which in Russian means "majority." Once the so-called majority within the RSDLP took over, they destroyed freedom of religion, speech, press, and assembly, and spread their bloody reign of terror throughout Russia. Notice how Lenin used words like social, democratic, and labor, or how Hitler used the word Nazi or the National Socialist German Workers' Party. These socialist tyrants manipulated words to fool the people and destroy freedom.

So while much of the misuse of the words democracy and republic is not done with malicious forethought, since they are erroneously used as synonyms, there has been in past history by tyrants and by a number of radical elements in America today, the purposeful manipulative abuse and misuse of language to distort our understanding of our Republican government structure that truly protects the people's God-given rights of life and liberty.

In like manner, a number of decent citizens find themselves mixing and marching in tandem with radical manipulators of American culture and politics. It is not a coincidence that during my experiences at both the "Walker is Hitler" rallies held by the Radical Left in early 2011, and the Loony*-Left "Occupy" rallies in the fall of 2011 and spring of 2012, many of the protestors were passionate apostles of a politically correct but historically incorrect and unconstitutional strict separation of God from government, and were advocates of democracy not republicanism. Many of them were members and/or supporters of the God-hating ACLU and Freedom From Religion Foundation out of Madison, Wisconsin. Unfortunately, a large number of decent Americans are involved with these rallies that comprise a large number of God-hating and God-denying anarchists, atheists, communists,

---

*I have been told by a few of my opponents that I lose credibility when I use the term "loony" to describe the radicals on the left wing of the political spectrum. But when you analyze some of the ideas the Radical Lefties advocate, I can think of no better word to describe them, as the dictionary defines "loony" as "extremely foolish or silly," and extreme, foolish, and silly is exactly what we see at these mobocrat marches.

and socialists who call for radical change and the transformation of our Republic under God.

It's a shame that President Obama, who considers himself a Christian, and many Democrats and teachers who claim to have a Christian faith, have endorsed, ignored, and/or failed to denounce and fight those radical elements within those twin mobocrat movements that have attached themselves to the Democratic Party. Far too many Americans go along with the mob or pretend not to know the villainous nature of the mob for political power, money, and vested interests.

And unfortunately many are the mob!

How did we get to this point in our country where many decent, kind, law-abiding people have joined in solidarity with radical, anti-republican elements that desire to destroy the very freedoms that they purport to defend? How is it that so many good teachers who are members of the Democratic Party have been duped into aligning themselves with such militant, radical, and loony left-wing elements? The Democratic Party of today is not the Democratic Party of my World War II veteran father Joseph Jacobs who was a true GI Joe. David Horowitz, a one-time '60s Marxist radical, has written a book called *Shadow Party: How George Soros, Hillary Clinton, and Sixties Radicals Seized Control of the Democratic Party.* The Amazon.com description of Horowitz's book is:

> America is under attack. Its institutions and values are under daily assault. But the principal culprits are not foreign terrorists. They are influential and powerful Americans secretly stirring up disunion and disloyalty

in the shifting shadows of the Democratic Party. New York Times best-selling authors David Horowitz and Richard Poe (both former radicals) weave together riveting history, investigative reporting, and cutting political analysis to help expose and explain:

The Shadow Party's plan to rewrite the U.S. Constitution.

How the Shadow Party overthrows foreign governments— and why it may attempt to use the same methods here.

The vast network of private think tanks, foundations, unions, stealth PACs, and other front groups through which the Shadow Party operates in America.

The network's voluminous contributions to the Democrats, which totaled more than $300 million in the 2004 elections, and its growing influence over the party's message and policy.

Why is it that so many within the Democratic Party have an unholy alliance with such anti-American, anti-Israel, anti-free-enterprise, and anti-republic-under-God groups?

The answer lies in history.

The history of collectivism, statism, Marxism, and socialism as manifested in their various anti-republican forms, are known today as "cultural Marxism." Karl Marx and Friedrich Engels believed that for their absolute "scientific socialism" to work, and for their historical determinism to succeed, the implementation of "democracy would be the road to socialism" and socialism would be the path to communism.

And communism would be the ultimate earthly paradise with eternal freedom, equality, peace on earth, and goodwill towards all.

To discover that road and how it is that many Americans and Democrats have been duped by its lies, let's turn to the history of cultural Marxism.

CHAPTER 4

CULTURAL MARXISM

"The first battlefield is the rewriting of history."
-Karl Marx

"Whatever we once were, we are no longer a Christian
nation at least, not just. We are also a Jewish nation, a
Muslim nation, a Buddhist nation, and a Hindu nation,
and a nation of nonbelievers."
-Barack Obama

What does cultural Marxism, the manipulation of language, and the misuse and misunderstanding of the word democracy have to do with a public school teacher in Midwest-America Wisconsin, where the cows are plenty, the Green Bay Packers are thirteen-time NFL world champs, and it snows like crazy?

Everything!

Why is it that in my twenty-four-year teaching career in Wisconsin public schools, I was always aware that at any moment my administrator might come into my classroom to ask why it is I taught this or that particular topic or subject that way? The administrator came in many times.

Karl Marx and political correctness is the answer.

How do we go from a dead German Jewish atheist who created one of the bloodiest philosophies the world has ever seen to political correctness in a Wisconsin classroom?

Easy. The Culture.

We know that the culture of our Republic under God in the early days of the United States was Judeo-Christian. In fact, America was predominately and primarily Judeo-Christian until the 1960s. What occurred to cause many teachers to give in to the powers that be so as to not cause a stir, rock the boat, or lose their jobs? Or why is it that many teachers throughout America teach their subject matter in a politically correct manner at the expense of historical context and truth?

A number of times in my public school teaching career I was reprimanded, taken to task, disciplined, or taken to the woodshed for daring to cross the politically correct line of demarcation between historical truth and the "party line" dictation of curriculum in my public school classroom. In my classroom my students were confronted with something they were not used to seeing, hearing or learning in their high school career:

God. Faith. Constitutional republicanism. Limited government.

And yes, unlike many left-wing teachers in America, I was as much an anti-communist as I was an anti-Nazi, and my students knew it!

I always wondered what it was like to be in biology class where they were taught that man was only a higher-order animal evolved from primordial goo, and then to walk into my classroom where they saw Harry S. Truman's 1949 inaugural quote written to confront Soviet Socialism's atheism. Truman makes reference to the book of Genesis chapter one where he boldly states:

> We believe that all men are created equal because they are created in the image of God. From this faith we will not be moved.

Or when they saw my President Kennedy quote. In confronting the cosmology of the Soviet Communists, Kennedy makes reference to the book of Exodus, where he says in his 1962 inaugural address that "the rights of man come not from the generosity of the State but from the hand of God."

In many of my students' classes they were taught that man was only mud, material, matter in motion, and created by accident in the evolutionary process. When they came into my room they learned just the opposite: They learned they were made in the image of God and by His hand!

Why?

Because I was simply teaching American history, European history, and social studies within a historical context while ignoring or defying the restraints of political correctness.

Why is it that at the Wisconsin school that I taught at for twenty-three years, the 1957 yearbook would quote Exodus 20:10, "to honor thy mother and father," but the yearbooks of the '70s through today would never dream of invoking God or quoting the Bible, the book that our presidents are sworn in on?

The answer is *Culture.*

Marxist, secular humanistic, progressive, Fabian, socialistic, anarchistic, atheistic, democratic, mobocratic culture.

Karl Marx may have died in 1883, but he lives on in many manifestations throughout the world today. His disciples or offshoots thereof have, over the past 130 years, altered and manipulated the language and ideas of America's Founders. That manipulation continues today as millions of Americans, through the influence of government schools at the high school and college level, are being taught various forms of politically correct cultural Marxism.

This progressive, socialist, communist, and secular humanist indoctrination is constantly being reinforced and blasted into our children's worldview by an equally politically correct media and morally corrupt Hollywood. This indoctrination, hidden under the guise of tolerance and multiculturalism, is always at the expense of our Republic under God.

But you might say:

"Hey wait, Dr. Jacobs! Karl Marx called for a 'dictatorship of the proletariat', a militant worldwide workers revolution where the have-nots—the proletariat—justly take from the haves—the unjust bourgeoisie. The movements you describe are not militant and certainly don't comprise the vast majority of the workers of America."

You are right. Marx was wrong.

While some of Marx's disciples like Vladimir Lenin, Leon Trotsky, Joseph Stalin, Mao Zedong, Ho Chi Minh, Kim Il-Sung,

Fidel Castro, and Che Guevara used militant means to murder well over one hundred million people in the twentieth century, many of his disciples, variants, and offshoots have reinterpreted his so-called "scientific socialism" in cultural terms. This cultural Marxism has manifested itself today in many of America's major institutions through organizations like the American Civil Liberties Union, the Freedom From Religion Foundation, Progressives for Obama, Students for a Democratic Society, Progressive Democrats of America, Congressional Progressive Caucus, Center for American Progress, Green for All, Midwest Academy, Congressional Black Caucus, Democratic Socialists of America, Workers Family Party, and myriads more radical groups that are undermining our republican form of government.

Many of these "community and scholastic socialists," through very subtle and strategic means, are transforming Marx's militant scientific socialism into "stealth socialism," fooling unsuspecting new recruits into believing they have joined a true democratic movement of social justice and income equality. Stealth socialism would not, for the most part, invoke Marx's name or use terms like Marxism, dialectic, and dictatorship of the proletariat, but would call for fairness, income equality, and social justice. Before we explain this clever, clandestine, covert communism we need to discuss some aspects of the more overt communist expressions of the late 1800s and the 1900s.

Some in the Marxist movements felt ashamed of covert stealth tactics, not due to any ethical convictions, but to their prideful true-believer mindset that Marx was right and they had nothing to hide. They proudly used his name, quoted the *Communist Manifesto* or *Das Capital*, utilized his terminology, and taught his philosophy openly and unabashedly. When the Russian Marxist Vladimir Lenin created the Comintern in 1919, he envisioned an international communist organization that would fight "by all available means, including armed force, for the overthrow of the international bourgeoisie and for the creation of an international Soviet republic as a transition stage to the complete abolition of the State." One available means to do this was to invite communist and socialist organizations from around the world to discuss and disseminate Marx's goal of a godless paradise.

Of the fifty-two delegates from the thirty-four parties worldwide, three popular American socialist groups that attended were the Socialist Labor Party of America (SLP), the International Workers of the World (IWW), and the Workers International Industrial Union (WIIU). These were some of the "useful idiots" Lenin ridiculed behind their backs, knowing he would use them as pawns in his international communist chess game.

These three organizations, like Marx, Lenin, and all socialist-communist organizations, could not have cared less for "the workers." The workers were a means to an end. The IWW, for example, unlike legitimate American labor unions, cared little for employer concessions to employees, as they in totalitarian fashion insisted on "society-transforming" demands instead of workplace improvement conditions. Many within the IWW called themselves the

"Red IWW" as they flew their communist red flags and sang from their *Little Red Songbook* that made parodies of Christian hymns for the workers like "Hallelujah I'm a Bum" or "Solidarity Forever." The IWW, unlike the Fabians, did not hide their solidarity with the violent and militant Soviet Socialists. Other groups like the Socialist Labor Party, Socialist Democratic Party, and Socialist Party of America, under either pseudoscientific pretensions or bogus democratic lingo, advocated or went along with extreme crazy ideas such as eugenics, the breeding of a superior race at the expense of the elimination of inferior races, and phrenology, the measurement of the human skull to determine superior human beings. It is not an accident that Margaret Sanger, a member of the Socialist Party and founder of Planned Parenthood, was a racist and passionate advocate of eugenics and the forced sterilization and eventual elimination of the Negro race. After all, the social-ists need to "transform society." You won't find this ugly socialist history on Planned Parenthood's baby-killing website. Other crazy, socialistic, anti-Constitutional ideas of the early 1900s called for the abolition of the Senate, the Presidency, state police forces, and the U.S. military.

Within the bizarre world of socialism—European style and American style—is the pretense of being a movement of workers for the workers, when in most cases it was a movement about the so-called workers but not of the workers. Karl Marx was not a "worker"; he was a writer who leeched and mooched off of others his whole life. Friedrich Engels was not a worker; he was a spoiled English aristocrat whose daddy paid his way through life.

The overwhelming majority of the movers and shakers in the various communist and socialist organizations were bourgeois intellectuals from affluent, prosperous backgrounds. They usually had the means to relax, read, and dream of a godless paradise that was always on paper for the workers and never for themselves.

Why did American Socialism fail to succeed in winning the masses in the first half of the twentieth century in the way that it attracted many in Europe and around the world?

With America's republican form of government early on, we had no titled aristocracy, no strict class structure, and no history of bloody class warfare of the haves versus the have-nots. Yes, we had the poor, but in America many of the poor were free and able to move up the social strata and achieve much more than Europe's societal schemes ever offered them. When European socialist immigrants preached their European Socialism to Americans, the overwhelming majority rejected their pie-in-the-sky collectivism, because in America, the reality was that factory workers didn't want to kill their bosses—they wanted to be the bosses; farmers didn't want to have the State take their land—they wanted to expand their property and prosper.

America's free-enterprise success sealed overt socialism's fate. Our Republic under God, coupled with the free market, created the most prosperous, socially mobile, and free society the world had ever seen. America's workers enjoyed a standard of living that by far exceeded most in European countries.

With migration possibilities in western America, most workers even during hard times saw their freedom as a better option to live a better life than the utopian militancy offered by many of the socialists, anarchists, and communists. Most Americans were content to work within the traditional two-party system where compromise spared bloodshed and revolution in the streets, as experienced in Europe. Additionally, socialists spend tremendous amounts of time and energy on fighting labor unions and attacking fellow socialists over nuanced interpretations of Marx, Engels, Lenin, and Trotsky, and like the Occupy movement of 2011, they were all over the place with a myriad of half-cocked ideas, silly schemes, and no concrete answers or solutions to improving society except to "Eat the Rich" and take their property.

The network of Marxist-socialists was unified in a few salient areas: their hatred of our Republic under God, free enterprise, limited government, and private ownership of property, and their desire to see the State control our lives. Americans could easily see what socialists were against, but never could understand what they were for, except the tearing down of society and the destruction of our republican way of life. It is not a coincidence that Americans overwhelmingly celebrate Labor Day in September distinctly different from the socialist, communist, and anarchist May Day red-flag-flying celebrations. In many cases the overt

Marxist groups, if allowed to, would join in solidarity with the covert stealth socialists having a common enemy:

Our Republic under God.

The roots of socialism in America can be traced to the arrival of German immigrants in the 1850s. Some of the German refugees were radicals who brought with them the fresh ideas of the German Karl Marx's 1848 *Communist Manifesto*. These immigrants started Marxian socialist unions such as the National Typographic Union in 1852, United Hatters of 1856, and Iron Molders' Union of North America in 1859. The Socialist Party in America grew immensely in the early 1900s under the dynamic leadership of Eugene V. Debs, and by 1912, socialist candidates won seats as 160 councilmen, 145 aldermen, 1 congressman, and 56 mayors, including Berkeley, California; Schenectady, New York; and Milwaukee, Wisconsin. Debs, who ran for president of the United States several times, was a staunch supporter of the militant Marxist-Russian revolutionaries Vladimir Lenin and Leon Trotsky. Debs served a sentence for sedition in the Atlanta Penitentiary (April 1919 to December 1921) where he said:

> Before serving time here, I made a series of addresses supporting the Russian revolution, which I consider the greatest single achievement in all history. I am still a Bolshevik. I am fighting for the same thing here they are fighting for there. I would go to jail again, yes, I would even go to the gallows for this cause.

Debs edited a bi-monthly magazine called The Class Struggle: Devoted to International Socialism. In his February 1919 issue, his article titled "The Day of The People," expressed his admiration for Lenin and Trotsky and how he was proud of being a Marxist:

> Lenin and Trotsky were the men of the hour and under their fearless, incorruptible and uncompromising leadership the Russian proletariat has held the fort against the combined assaults of all the ruling class powers of earth. It is a magnificent spectacle. It stirs the blood and warms the heart of every revolutionist, and it challenges the admiration of all the world.
>
> The people are ready for their day. THE PEOPLE, I say. Yes, the people! Who are the people? The people are the working class, the lower class, the robbed, the oppressed, the impoverished, the great majority of the earth. They and those who sympathize with them are THE PEOPLE, and they who exploit the working class, and the mercenaries and menials who aid and abet the exploiters, are the enemies of the people... our valiant comrades are leading the proletarian revolution, which knows no race, no color, no sex, and no boundary lines. They are setting the heroic example for worldwide emulation. Let us, like them, scorn and repudiate the cowardly compromisers within our own ranks, challenge and defy the robber-class power, and fight it out on that line to victory or death!
>
> From the crown of my head to the soles of my feet I am Bolshevik, and proud of it.
>
> The Day of the People has arrived!

The Marxist Eugene V. Debs was a frequent lecturer on American college campuses through the auspices of the Intercollegiate Socialist Society (ISS). The ISS was a socialist student organization from 1905 to 1921 that very carefully crafted its Marxist ideas with the language of democracy and social justice. It was comprised of many prominent intellectuals and writers such as John Dewey, Upton Sinclair, Clarence Darrow, Jack London, and Graham Phelps Stokes, among others. It is relevant to note that one of its most famous members, Clarence Darrow, was the ACLU lawyer for the infamous Scopes Monkey Trial of 1925, where Darrow's Darwinian worldview made an attempt to ridicule the Bible and its use in America's public schools.

The ISS acted as the unofficial Socialist Party of America student wing and had branches at the University of Wisconsin-Madison, the University of Michigan, the University of California-Berkeley, and sixty other colleges from New York to California. The ISS produced socialist magazines and sponsored lecture tours and seminars all over the U.S. aimed at propagating Marxist-Socialist ideas among America's young college men and women, where they discussed the "New Gospel according to St. Marx." Universities were considered to be fertile soil to plant the seeds of progressive, socialist, and communist thought. The ISS developed a broader stealth philosophy in the 1920s that did not deal solely with college students but expanded its emphasis on leaders throughout America in government, newspapers, radio, television, and Hollywood. To symbolize the shift in emphasis, the group changed its name from

ISS to LID, the League for Industrial Democracy. Co-director Norman Thomas told the New York Times in 1919 that the ISS was created to "throw light on the worldwide movement of industrial democracy known as socialism." Another motivation for the ISS name change was that by 1921, the militant and violent nature of the USSR caused many closet Marxists, or socialists, to substitute the word socialism for democracy. Stealth socialism's understanding of the word democracy added a clever twist to its original and historical meaning. They very astutely mixed Marxian concepts into the fabric of the word democracy.

Their new definition of democracy conveyed the idea of the State taking over all the nation's resources and the means of production and distribution, and of ultimately giving "power to the people" to control society in totality, otherwise known as totalitarianism. This very clever lingual alchemy used the tyrannical aspects of democracy under the guise of the positive aspects of democracy, i.e., the people are "free" to participate in a "free" society where theoretically all the people have the power to control all of life.

At this time there were conservative elements in America that understood this subterfuge and perversion of language and spoke out against it. For example, the 1928 U.S. Army Training Manual No. 2000-25 had a whole section teaching on the historical difference between a legitimate constitutional republic and an illegitimate tyrannical democracy. Bob Hardison writes this in his Barefoot blog:

Training Manual No. TM 2000-25 on Citizenship, U.S. History and the Constitution was compiled and issued by the U.S. War Department, November 30, 1928, to teach our young men in the services the fundamental principles upon which our Government was founded. The precise and scholarly definitions presented throughout the manual were carefully considered as a proper guide for U.S. soldiers and U.S. citizens by the Chief of Staff of the United States Army. Such definitions take precedence over any definitions that may be found in the present commercial dictionaries, which have suffered periodic modification to please the powers in office.

Shortly after the "bank holiday" in 1933, orders from the FDR White House suddenly demanded without explanation that all copies of this book be withdrawn from the Government Printing Office and the Army posts, to be suppressed and destroyed. So began the demagogic descent of the United States and the subversion of the Constitution into Americanized National Socialism.

The 1928 U.S. Army Training Manual properly defines democracy this way:

Democracy: A government of the masses. Authority derived through mass meeting or any other form of "direct" expression. Results in mobocracy.

Attitude toward property is communistic—negating property rights.

Attitude toward law is that the will of the majority shall regulate, whether it be based upon deliberation or governed by passion, prejudice, and impulse, without restraint or regard to consequences.

Results in demagoguism, license, agitation, discontent, anarchy.

I quote the 1928 U.S. Army Training Manual extensively because of its keen insight into our Founders' understanding of a republican form of government:

Republic: Authority is derived through the election by the people of public officials best fitted to represent them.

Attitude toward property is respect for laws and individual rights, and a sensible economic procedure.

Attitude toward law is the administration of justice in accord with fixed principles and established evidence, with a strict regard to consequences. A greater number of citizens and extent of territory may be brought within its compass. Avoids the dangerous extreme of either tyranny or mobocracy. Results in statesmanship, liberty, reason, justice, contentment, and progress.

A republic is a form of government under a constitution which provides for the election of (1) an executive and (2) a legislative body, who working together in a representative capacity, have all the power of appointment, all power of legislation, all power to raise revenue and appropriate expenditures, and are required to create (3) a judiciary to pass upon the justice and legality of their governmental acts and to recognize (4) certain inherent individual rights.

Take away any one or more of those four elements and you are drifting into autocracy. Add one or more to those four elements and you are drifting into democracy. — Atwood.

121. Superior to all others. — Autocracy declares the divine right of kings; its authority can not be questioned; its powers are arbitrarily or unjustly administered.

Democracy is the "direct" rule of the people and has been repeatedly tried without success. Our Constitutional fathers, familiar with the strength and weakness of both autocracy and democracy, with fixed principles definitely in mind, defined a representative republican form of government. They "made a very marked distinction between a republic and a democracy and said repeatedly and emphatically that they had founded a republic."

James Madison, in The Federalist Papers, emphasized the fact that this government was a republic and not a democracy, the Constitution makers having considered both an autocracy and a democracy as undesirable forms of government while "a republic promises the cure for which we are seeking."

"In a democracy the people meet and exercise the government in person. In a republic they assemble and administer it by their respective agents." —James Madison.

"The advantage which a republic has over a democracy consists in the substitution of representatives whose enlightened views and virtuous sentiments render them superior to local prejudices and to schemes of injustice." —James Madison.

The American form of government is the oldest republican form of government in the world, and is exercising a pronounced influence in modifying the governments of other nations. Our Constitution has been copied in whole or in part throughout the earth.

122. No direct action. Under the representative form of government there is no place for "direct action." The inherent characteristic of a republic is government by representation. The people are permitted to do only two things: they may vote once every four years for the Executive and they may vote once every two years for members of the legislative body.

FDR's 1933 "unexplained" removal of the 1928 U.S. Army Training Manual can be explained in light of his socialistic New Deal programs that needed to undermine our republican form of government in order to pass their big government social welfare state programs. The demagogic, socialistic descent, although not started by FDR, was certainly accelerated by him.

By the end of World War II, most Americans were not fooled by the blatant and overt use of the word socialism and the misuse of the word democracy, especially with socialism's bloody reign of terror in Europe. Nazis were, in reality, National Socialists; Soviets were, in reality, Soviet Socialists; and there were numerous socialist parties throughout Europe that desired to destroy the Judeo-Christian heritage of the European nations. European Socialists had so bastardized and twisted the words democracy and republic that Americans for the most part were not fooled by their linguistic lies. It is relevant to note that ISS's Norman

Thomas ran for president of the United States six times on the Socialist Party ticket, and he is reported to have said:

> The American people will never knowingly adopt socialism, but under the name of liberalism they will adopt every fragment of the socialist program until one day America will be a socialist nation without ever knowing how it happened.

While historians debate whether Thomas actually said the above, the stealth spirit of it applies to the manipulative and nefarious nature of Marxism and its variants. Americans for the most part did not buy into the form of government that the Marxists or the socialists of various stripes and calibers were selling.

How is it, then, that cultural Marxism succeeded in infiltrating America where militant Marxism failed? That will be the topic of our next chapter.

CHAPTER 5

FABIANS

"Beware of false prophets who come disguised as harmless sheep but are really vicious wolves."
-Matthew 7:15

"Socialism only works in two places: Heaven where
they don't need it and hell where they already have it."
-Ronald Reagan

Who were the Fabians?

The Fabian Society, which favored gradual evolutionary change rather than revolutionary change, was named in honor of the Roman general Fabius Maximus (nicknamed Cunctator, meaning "the Delayer"). His strategy advocated tactics of harassment and attrition rather than head-on battles against the Carthaginian army under the revered general Hannibal. An explanatory note appearing on the title page of the Society's first pamphlet declared:

> For the right moment you must wait, as Fabius did most patiently, when warring against Hannibal, though many censured his delays; but when the time comes you must strike hard, as Fabius did, or your waiting will be in vain, and fruitless.

In reality, here is what they meant:

> For the right moment you must wait, be patient Marxist-Socialists when warring against Christian Western Civilization and America's Republic under God; when the right time comes we will strike like Fabius and defeat England, America, and the world; your waiting will not have be in vain or fruitless.

The Fabians did not create a political party but utilized the clever strategy of "socialistic 'permeation' of existing political institutions." Margaret Cole, as a proud former head of the British Fabian Society, in her book, *The Story of Fabian Socialism*, gives interesting details of the character of the early Fabians:

> The handful who made up the Fabian society, only forty in 1885, were as vaguely anarchistic and insurrectionist in their ideas and their expression of them as any group that had existed before them. They regularly denounced capitalists as thieves and talked about using dynamite, and they looked forward with confidence to an imminent social revolution, to take place somewhere about 1889.

Cole goes on to say that "the Fabians were a 'seeding' body busily sowing socialist schemes throughout society and then nursing them into full bloom."

The prolific atheist writer George Bernard Shaw became a Fabian in 1884. Shaw showed the difference between other militant and radical Marxist and socialist groups and his own group by repeated references to "the highly respectable Fabian Society." He illustrates the tactic of being "highly respectable" as follows:

The Fabian Society got rid of its Anarchists and Borrovians, and presented Socialism in the form of a series of parliamentary measures, thus making it possible for an ordinary respectable religious citizen to profess socialism and belong to a Socialist Society without any suspicion of lawlessness, exactly as he might profess himself a Conservative and belong to an ordinary constitutional club.

The Fabians were excellent at creating a facade of respectability, while at the same time infiltrating society for revolutionary purposes. The Fabians were more cunning and realistic than the overtly Marxist-Socialists. They were convinced that it is much easier to fool the children and wives of the rich and influential than it is to convince the working classes. They also understood that while Marx called for a mass movement from the working class, the Fabians focused on the middle and upper classes. Shaw describes the social composition of the Fabians:

> Now the significant thing about the particular Socialist society, which I joined, was that the members all belonged to the middle class. Indeed, its leaders and directors belonged to what is sometimes called the upper-middle class: that is, they were either professional men like myself (I had escaped from clerkdom into literature) or members of the upper division of the civil service. Several of them have since had distinguished careers without changing their opinions or leaving the Society. To their Conservative and Liberal parents and aunts and uncles fifty years ago it seemed an amazing, shocking, unheard-of thing that they should become Socialists, and also a

step bound to make an end of all their chances of success in life. Really it was quite natural and inevitable. Karl Marx was not a poor laborer: he was the highly educated son of a rich Jewish lawyer. His almost equally famous colleague, Friedrich Engels, was a well-to-do employer. It was precisely because they were liberally educated, and brought up to think about how things are done instead of merely drudging at the manual labor of doing them, that these two men, like my colleagues in The Fabian Society (note, please, that we gave our society a name that could have occurred only to classically educated men), were the first to see that Capitalism was reducing their own class to the condition of a proletariat, and that the only chance of securing anything more than a slave's share in the national income for anyone but the biggest capitalists or the cleverest professional or business men lay in a combination of all the proletarians, without distinction of class or country to put an end to capitalism by developing the communistic side of our civilization until communism became the dominant principle in society, and mere owning, profiteering, and genteel idling were disabled and discredited.

Shaw joined the Fabian Society hoping to create "a new communistic world order." Shaw's raw and vile Fabianism can be seen for what it is when he writes:

Under Socialism, you would not be allowed to be poor. You would be forcibly fed, clothed, lodged, taught, and employed whether you liked it or not. If it were discovered that you had not character and industry enough to be worth all this trouble, you might possibly be executed in a kindly manner; but whilst you were permitted to live, you would have to live well.

Shaw's socialism wouldn't tolerate the natural by-product of socialism's track record to date: laziness, indolence, and mooching. He would simply use the State to eliminate such elements.

It is not a coincidence that in spite of their facade of respectability, the Fabians consorted with their more militant comrades in Russia as they aided and abetted Russian Marxists at least a decade before the 1917 Russian Revolution.

Fabian Window

There could not be a more appropriate image to represent cultural Marxism than the Fabian coat of arms of a wolf in sheep's clothing as pictured on the previous page.

The Fabian window was designed by George Bernard Shaw and depicts Sydney Webb and Shaw striking the earth with hammers to "REMOULD IT NEARER TO THE HEART'S DESIRE," a line from Persian philosopher Omar Khayyam. The window is now on display at the London School of Economics, which was founded by Sydney and Beatrice Webb.

Across the bottom of the window, the masses kneel in worship before a stack of books advocating the theories of socialism. To the left at the bottom, thumbing his nose at the docile masses, is H.G. Wells who, after quitting the Fabians, denounced them as "the new Machiavellians." It is not a coincidence that the Fabian Society was originally founded in 1883, the year of Karl Marx's death. Marx may have died but his ideas did not. The Fabians were hell-bent on promoting his ideas. The Fabians' goal was to mold the earth nearer to their hearts' desire.

The early Fabians were all passionate in their denial of the God of Abraham, Isaac, and Jacob, and His revelation in the Scriptures. While they rejected historic-orthodox Christianity, they used liberal Christian ministers to advance their cause.

The Fabians chose the written word, politics, and education to persuade people of the need for transformational change in the major institutions of society. Leading Fabians penetrated political parties, government offices, labor unions, schools, the press, and

Parliament by obtaining influential positions in these institutions. The first changes in English society were made in the schools.

Victorian England's Judeo-Christian worldview saw education as a way to develop in each individual a Christian mind that would be used for the glory of God. Like neo-liberalism, progressivism, and the other new philosophies of the twentieth century, Fabianism called for a new non-Christian philosophy of education. Fabians espoused an anti-biblical education that ignored the sinful nature and fall of man, while students were taught that mankind's problems were caused by outward societies, not the inward sinful man; therefore, society had to be remade in order to create a new world.

The goal of this new stealth socialistic education in the social evolutionary process was to adjust the individual to his environment so the State could control the child for the sake of the welfare of society. Fabian-Socialistic education became the tool used to destroy Judeo-Christian traditional values in order to prepare the British people for socialism's eventual goal of communism. The State centralization of education would be utilized to control curriculum and teaching methods in order to achieve the goal of socialization.

In 1906, the British Labour Party adopted for its permanent party platform a Fabian study entitled Labour and the New Social Order. It proposed what it called "The Four Pillars of the House":

1. A national minimum wage and state-financed social welfare program;

2. Government control of land, utilities, transportation, mining, and heavy industry;

3. Abolition of private savings and private investment through confiscatory taxation;

4. Disarmament, an international court, international economic controls, international social legislation, and an international One-World authority.

Many of these "pillars" were later incorporated into the League of Nations and even later into the United Nations.

Besides George Bernard Shaw, many of the early Fabian members were famous atheists and anti-Christian writers and philosophers like H.G. Wells, Bertrand Russell, Julius Huxley, Aldous Huxley, and John Maynard Keynes.

H.G. Wells, a devout Darwinian atheist who advocated extreme forms of eugenics, or race purification, wrote of and envisioned what he called a "World State," where the State, in godlike fashion, would end poverty, greed, social injustice, and inferior races.

The preeminent philosopher and atheist of his day and an early Fabian member was Bertrand Russell who, like Wells and Shaw, looked for the State to replace God in order to usher in peace and justice.

Fabian Aldous Huxley wrote the dystopian novel *Brave New World*, while his brother, Julian Huxley, became the first head of the United Nations Educational, Scientific, and Cultural Organization (UNESCO), where he laid a socialist foundation—the global education program—now being implemented around the world. Julian wrote in his 1947 UN address:

Further, since the world today is in process of becoming one, and since a major aim of UNESCO must be to help in the speedy and satisfactory realization of this process... UNESCO must pay special attention to international education—to education as a function of a world society, in addition to its function in relation to national societies, to regional or religious or intellectual groups or to local communities.

Twenty years earlier in 1927, Fabian Julian Huxley published *Religion Without Revelation*, where he ridicules the ancient Judeo-Christian presupposition that the LORD God revealed Himself in the Scriptures to mankind through Abraham, Isaac, Jacob, Moses, and Jesus.

Wells, Shaw, Russell, Aldous Huxley, Julian Huxley, and other Fabian intellectuals had a diabolical strategy to seduce the people into bowing down and worshiping the learning of man and his false philosophies that are anti-Christian and anti-American republicanism. The stealth Fabian-socialist agenda has been moving slowly but steadily forward for well over one hundred years as its adherents hammer away at forging their utopian vision of a so-called free, equal, and classless society. Their symbol of a turtle conveys their slow but steady pace in the race to beat the militant Marxist hare.

Professor Maurice Cranston of the London School of Economics writes:

Fabianism flourished when the double impact of WWI and the Great Depression had destroyed many other illusions. In spite of its claim to be a form of socialism, Fabianism became assimilated by liberals, as liberalism took on the ideas of state regulation of the economy, bureaucratic planning, income transfers to relieve poverty, and the subordination of civil and political rights to so-called social and economic rights. This is as true of American as of English liberals, despite America's deep traditional attachment to economic freedom.

Fabianism started out in England in education, then worked its way into politics and the media, and has been profoundly successful in destroying much of Great Britain's Christian civilization. What National Socialism or Soviet Socialism could not do—to quote Winston Churchill, "destroy Christian civilization"—Fabian stealth socialism has done culturally within a few generations.

This author has seen, heard, felt, and experienced firsthand the death of Christian England in the last thirty years. I did undergraduate work in education in 1980 at the University of Brighton, while teaching at a local English high school, and received my Ph.D. in London, England, in 1998. My wife and I have given historical tours to England for twenty years, and every time we go we comment on how England has drifted from her Judeo-Christian beginnings. The same is happening in America.

Aaron Klein writes in his book, *Red Army: The Radical Network That Must Be Defeated To Save America*:

The so-called socialist permeation began slowly near the end of the nineteenth century, when Fabian Society leaders came from England to the United States to train groups in the "art of socialism." The Fabians have fooled many "ordinary respectable religious citizens" into becoming "Star-Spangled Socialists."

Unfortunately, the last bastion of Christian civilization in the world today—our Republic under God—has gone in the same Fabian direction. Slowly but steadily, Fabian Society leaders migrated from England to America to indoctrinate groups in the "art of socialism." Like the ISS, the Fabians had a profound impact on many American colleges such as Harvard, Columbia, Brown, and the University of Wisconsin-Madison.

While Joseph Stalin's USSR was never able to turn the USA into a communist nation through military means, Stalin did understand the spirit of the Fabians when he stated:

> America is like a healthy body and its resistance is three-fold: its patriotism, its morality, and its spiritual life. If we can undermine these three areas, America will collapse from within.

Since the 1960s in America, the Marxist-Fabian "Trojan horse" of collapse from within is boring its way through our societal institutions. Dwight Eisenhower's Secretary of Agriculture, Ezra Taft Benson, told his Brigham Young University crowd in 1968:

> I have talked face to face with the godless communist leaders. It may surprise you to learn that I was host to Mr. Khrushchev for a half day when he visited the United States. As we talked face to face, he indicated that my grandchildren would live under communism.

After assuring him that I expected to do all in my power to assure that his and all other grandchildren will live under freedom he arrogantly declared in substance: "You Americans are so gullible. No, you won't accept communism outright, but we'll keep feeding you small doses of socialism until you'll finally wake up and find you already have communism. We won't have to fight you. We'll so weaken your economy until you'll fall like overripe fruit into our hands."

Nikita Khrushchev bombastically bragged how the communists and socialists were moving forward with their world agenda. Nikita stated that they would give Americans small doses of socialism until one day we would wake up and find we had communism, and then, he boasted, we would "fall like overripe fruit into their hands." While Khrushchev and the Soviet Socialists lost their overt militant Marxist war, they are winning battle after battle in the covert war of cultural Marxism.

These wolves in sheep's clothing have duped and seduced many in America through a gradual, evolutionary process rather than through an abrupt, violent revolutionary means.

Fabianism-cultural Marxism is a way for the apostles of Marxism to secretly bring about a post-modern age, a transformed America, a new world order. Their basic premise is that western civilization—American republicanism—will not accept militant Marxism, and so it must be subverted over a long period of time in order to be primed for the acceptance of a more covert form of communism. This subversion of western Christian culture would include the breakdown of the nuclear family and of biblical law and order, and usher in mass illegal immigration, radical feminism, and political correctness.

CHAPTER 6

ACLU: STEALTH
SOCIALISM AT ITS FINEST

> "I am for socialism, disarmament, and, ultimately, for
> abolishing the state itself... I seek the social owner-
> ship of property, the abolition of the propertied class,
> and the sole control of those who produce wealth.
> Communism is the goal."
> *-Roger Baldwin*

A classic example of stealth socialism or American Fabianism
and cultural Marxism is the American Civil Liberties Union
or the ACLU. The so-called "all-American" ACLU claims that it is
a purely non-partisan, objective organization that is "neither liberal
nor conservative, Republican nor Democrat," and is "devoted
exclusively to protecting the basic civil liberties of all Americans."
But the facts prove otherwise. From its very inception the ACLU
was an ideological chameleon that proclaimed it was a champion
of "truth, justice, and the American way," when all along its radical
atheistic agenda was contrary to the basic principles of American
constitutional republicanism.

Aaron Klein writes in his book, *Red Army: The Radical Network
That Must Be Defeated To Save America*:

ACLU co-founder Roger Baldwin advised a socialist agitator early in the twentieth century to "steer away from making it look like a Socialist enterprise" and to employ subterfuge tactics. Convince people of your American values by flying lots of American flags; talk about the Constitution and what the Founding Fathers wanted America to become, Baldwin says.

Who is this Roger Baldwin, a student of Fabian Socialism? Baldwin came from a family steeped in socialism and Unitarianism that denied the deity of Christ and professed a universal religious worldview that attacked the Bible as God's very words to man and Jesus as the only way to heaven. Baldwin denied the orthodox, biblical, Christian heritage of America's Founders and dedicated his life to the absolute separation of God from government. While wrapping themselves in the American flag, quoting our Founding Fathers, and feigning loyalty to the U.S., Baldwin's Fabian followers used tactics and stealth strategy that had the ultimate goal of circumventing our constitutional republican form of government by using the judiciary to override the legislative branch's prerogative and legitimate power to make the laws of the land. The original board members of the ACLU were a veritable who's who of radical anarchists, socialists, and communists such as Norman Thomas, six-time Socialist Party candidate for president; William Z. Foster, chairman of the Communist Party USA; Max Eastman, editor of the Communist Party's The Masses, and many, many more who maintained membership with dozens and dozens of communist organizations or Fabian front groups fooling Americans into believing they were friends of freedom. Unfortunately, from their inception in 1920 until today, they have been profoundly successful. From their landmark 1925 Scopes Monkey Trial victory to take the Bible out of government schools, to the 1973 baby-murdering Roe vs. Wade, the ACLU has been the secular Left's socialists frontline in destroying the Founders' vision of a Republic under God and traditional Christian family values. The ACLU, with their thousands of lawyers and their ideological ally, the National Education Association, have intimidated thousands of public school teachers across America into cowering in their classroom for fear that they might cross their Big-Brother political correctness and actually teach historical context and original intent. Numerous court cases won by the elite, arrogant ACLU lawyers have helped accelerate the destruction of traditional family values, while defending abnormal and perverted so-called families and lifestyles. From the North American Men Boys Love Association (NAMBLA) to Lesbian, Gay, Bisexual & Transgender (LGBT), the ACLU has defended the perversion of "liberties" with a license to sin with societal acceptance and pride. We should not be surprised that many of Roger Baldwin's close friends, heroes, and ideological soul mates were radical anarchists and socialists such as Margaret Sanger and Emma Goldman. Sanger, a eugenicist who advocated the forced government sterilization of the "inferior" Negro was the founder of Planned Parenthood, which works hand in hand with the ACLU to destroy life and liberty in this land. Sanger's friend and supporter in Planned Parenthood, Emma Goldman, or "Red Emma," who was an early supporter of the communist Vladimir Lenin, was an advocate of anarchism, abortion, free love, and complete separation of God from government. Baldwin affectionately called her the "Red Queen of Anarchy." Baldwin, who claimed to be a pacifist, was an admirer not only of Vladimir Lenin but of the communist dictator Joseph Stalin. After his 1927 visit to the Soviet Union, his 1928 book *Liberty Under the Soviets* gives an admiring and glowing account of Soviet Socialism, and while acknowledging "repressions in Soviet Russia," Baldwin justified them as necessary repressions or weapons to assist Stalin's dictatorship of the proletariat in the "transition period to socialism" and then our long-awaited "Paradise Communism."

Baldwin's duplicity in typical Orwellian "doublespeak" can be readily seen for what it is when he declared:

> I am for socialism, disarmament, and ultimately for
> abolishing the state itself as an instrument of violence
> and compulsion. I seek social ownership of property,
> the abolition of the propertied class, and sole control
> by those who produce wealth. Communism is the goal.

As a so-called pacifist, Baldwin was either naive or cunning, for while he used the rhetoric of "freedom," he advocated the violence of communism and the classic Marxian "dictatorship of the proletariat." In 1934, as director of the ACLU, Baldwin wrote an article titled "Freedom in the USA and the USSR." In the article he takes off his Fabian sheep's clothes to reveal his true wolf colors as he speaks of mass murderer Joseph Stalin's so-called "workers":

> But "workers democracy" in action is no product of coercion. It is genuine, and it is the nearest approach to freedom that the workers have ever achieved.

> How long the proletarian dictatorship will last, only world conditions and internal success in building socialism can determine. Highly centralized authority will give way. The State and police power will eventually disappear. Civil liberties will exist again, within the confines of a socialist society; but not to oppose it, for who will want to? The extension of education, the bringing up of a generation to take active responsibility all over the Soviet Union will lessen power at the center and from the top.

> If American workers, with no real liberties save to change masters or, rarely, to escape from the working class, could understand their class interests, Soviet "Workers' democracy" would be their goal. And if American champions of civil liberty could all think in terms of economic freedom as the goal of their labors, they too would accept "workers' democracy" as far superior to what the capitalist world offers to any but a small minority. Yes, and they would accept—regretfully, of course—the necessity of dictatorship while the job of reorganizing society on a socialist basis is being done.

I quoted Baldwin extensively here because it is a perfect example of the worldview and mindset of a clever, naïve, and stupid communist visionary.

Clever, naive, and stupid in the same man? Yes.

For a so-called intelligent Harvard graduate it was naïve to believe that "dictatorship and highly centralized authority will give way" and that "the State and police power will eventually disappear." By 1934, Joseph Stalin's Marxist ideas had murdered millions. It was clever to use terms like "workers' democracy," as many were duped by such rhetoric into believing that the ACLU did represent our Founders' vision of a proper form of democratic government to protect liberty. And Baldwin was stupid to declare that Soviet Marxism was "far superior to what the capitalist world" offered. In typical hypocritical fashion, Baldwin left the Soviet paradise and lived his life in the freest, most socially mobile and prosperous Republic under God that the world has ever seen, the United States of America.

Of course, defenders of ACLU's subterfuge will say Baldwin eventually kicked out the Stalinists within his organization. He did, because by the time the murdering communist cat was out of the bag, Baldwin was not only embarrassed for his naivety and stupidity, but he had to sanitize his presentation of "liberty" to continue his agenda of "communism as the goal." Another clever tactic employed by the ACLU under the guise of having a "diverse legal portfolio" is to occasionally leave its left-wing arena and defend conservative groups, and yet ideologically in 95 percent of its cases it sheds its "objectivity" to advance its radical left-wing causes. We need to understand the ideological nature of America's nefarious internal enemy. Roger Baldwin believed that the ACLU "Is a private organization, and a private organization is like a church. You don't take non-believers into the church. We are a church; we have a creed and only true believers should lead us."

The ACLU, "the Church of anti-Republic-under-God true believers," like all of us, has a worldview, a philosophical orientation and interpretation of life's origin, meaning, and ultimate purpose. America's Founders, like the vast majority of Americans today, presuppose the God of the Bible as the Supreme Being who created the heavens and earth. Roger Baldwin and his Socialist-Communist colleagues do not. To establish their anti-Christian worldview, their vision of what America ought to be, they have from the very beginning denied and lied about our republic's Christian foundation and philosophical orientation. Rabbi Spero, in his article, "The ACLU Enemy of America and Christianity," hits the bull's-eye when he writes:

> For we know what motivates the ACLU and what is its ultimate goal. Long ago it decided to do whatever it takes to expunge America of its affinity to Christianity and strip our society of its Judeo-Christian touchstone and foundation. It expanded the context of separation of church and state to accomplish this goal, and a good-willed citizenry acquiesced for they did not wish to question what they assumed were the pure, constitutional motivations behind the ACLU's campaign. Who wants to question an organization with beguiling head-banners such as American and Civil Liberties. The ACLU has manipulated church/state issues and used it selectively when it furthered its own anti-Christian agenda. Evidently, separation of church from state is not

the inviolable principle we were led to believe given the ACLU's own brushing aside of it if standing in the way of Islamic desires. For, truthfully, nothing would give the ACLU more pleasure than forcing upon America—and its students—a multi-culturalism and multi-religionism that would effectively diminish the influence and identity of America as a Judeo-Christian society.

When we observe and dialogue with the "Walker is Hitler" mob-ocrats in Madison, Wisconsin, or the "Eat the Rich" Occupy mob around the country, it is not surprising to see their comradeship and ideological kinship with the ACLU, as they both stem from the same "this is what democracy looks like" anti-republicanism worldview. Bill O'Reilly, in his 2006 book, *Cultural Warrior*, pegs the ACLU with astuteness when he writes:

> If you pay attention to the culture war, it is clear who the shock troops are: The American Civil Liberties Union (ACLU) is the vanguard, waging a war of legal maneu-vers designed to ensure secular policies without having to go to the ballot box. In the past 10 years thousands of ACLU lawsuits have blitzed the legal system, almost all of them designed to promote progressive causes and banish traditional ones.

Roger Baldwin, through deceptive language and legal acumen, created a bogus image of the ACLU being a liberty-protecting orga-nization when all along the ACLU has been undermining freedom in America. Incredulously, Baldwin was awarded by none other than Democratic President Jimmy Carter the Medal of Freedom in 1981. While Baldwin died a few months later in 1981, his goal of communism and the destruction of our Republic under God is right on course with ACLU lawyers leading the charge!

CHAPTER 7

GRAMSCI AND THE FRANKFURT SCHOOL

"Under the rule of a repressive whole, liberty can be made into a powerful instrument of domination."
-Herbert Marcuse

"The original strategy to destroy America, employed by the Frankfurt School, came from Italian Communist Antonio Gramsci who realized that in order to achieve a Socialist victory, cultural institutions would have to be infiltrated and subverted. Gramsci realized that America, steeped in traditions of freedom and liberty, would never succumb to a frontal assault..."
-Patrick Buchanan

Another great mind to advance cultural Marxism was Antonio Gramsci (1891–1937). Born in Sardinia, Gramsci studied philosophy at the University of Turin, and soon after he started the Italian Communist Party, he left Italy for the Soviet Union, fearing that ex-socialist-turned-fascist Benito Mussolini would imprison him. In the USSR, Gramsci challenged Marx's, Lenin's, and Stalin's dictatorship of the proletariat that was driven by economic determinism and the violent overthrow of the capitalist system. Gramsci argued that Marx's "worker's paradise" would never be achieved as long as Christianity had a hold on the people. He believed that rather than capitalism being the main enemy of

Marxism, it was Christianity and its control of culture in western civilization. Gramsci wrote that western civilization had been thoroughly infused with Christianity for 2,000 years and that the Judeo-Christian worldview remained the predominant ethical, moral, and philosophical system in Europe and North America.

Simply put: western civilization and Christianity were inextricably woven together and must be separated to achieve "Paradise Communism."

Gramsci observed that Christianity's cultural practices and moral persuasions were so much a part of the daily lives of nearly everyone in society, including non-Christians living in Christian lands, that it had established an almost impossible wall for Marxists to breach to create a Marxist utopia. Attempting to break down that Christian cultural wall proved next to impossible. Therefore, in place of a militant frontal attack, Gramsci taught that with a patient evolutionary pace and not with reactionary revolutionary violence, it was much more advantageous to attack the enemy's Christian society with slow, subtle, stealth strategies.

Time and the Fabian turtle were on their side.

What Gramsci called the "long march through the institutions" had the ultimate goal of grinding and transforming Christian society's collective mind gradually and progressively over a period of a few generations, thus deteriorating from within its former Christian worldview and changing it into one more in harmony with communism.

Additionally, unlike the militant Marxist-Leninists who were hostile towards the noncommunist left, Gramsci believed that comradeship with a variety of leftist groups would be a more effective strategy to achieve an ultimate communist victory. In Gramsci's day these included, trade unions, various anti-fascist organizations, and socialist political groups.

"In our day, alliances with the Left would include radical feminists, extremist environmentalists, civil rights movements, anti-police associations, internationalists, ultraliberal church groups," anti-Israel associations, trade and teachers' unions, progressives and major elements of the Democratic Party. These organizations, along with militant Marxists, create a unified front working for the transformation of the Judeo-Christian culture and society. This is why, whether it is the "Walker is Hitler" crowd in Madison or the Occupy "Capitalism is evil" crowd across America, this motley, multifaceted, discombobulated gang joins in solidarity against their common enemies:

Conservatives, Christians, and
Constitutional Republicans.

Gramsci advised Marxists to achieve power by "democratic means" and then to use it to destroy what he called Christian cultural hegemony. Gramsci's cultural hegemony consisted of the belief that Marxists must begin by influencing the culture through winning the intellectuals and the teachers, and by infiltrating the press, the media, and publishers.

Marxists had to create a culture that would infuse itself into every sphere of society and the body politic.

Gramsci returned to Mussolini's Italy and in 1926 he was imprisoned and spent the rest of his life in prison, dying there in 1937. He quickly became a martyr for the Marxist cause and his *Prison Notebooks*, in which he describes his covert plan to destroy western civilization and Christianity's hold on the culture, became a communist classic in the '60s and still is today for the Radical Left. In fact, his books were sold to the mob in Madison and are very popular with the Occupy crowd.

Radical Leftists in the United States, Europe, and Latin America have adopted Gramsci's methods and have made a point of infiltrating churches, universities, and media outlets. Ecumenical movements and peace and social justice commissions have grown through Gramsci's influence and have diminished and diluted basic Christian doctrines. University curricula reflecting Gramsci's ideas teach that all cultures must be equally respected except the Christian culture, which is marginalized, ostracized, and demonized by many college professors. In the name of human rights and social justice, secular humanist, socialist, and progressive organizations have promoted policies that have eliminated Judeo-Christian moral persuasion and restraints on the people.

Another influential cultural Marxist was Gramsci's contemporary comrade, Hungarian George Lukacs. In 1919, as deputy commissar for culture in Communist Hungary, Lukacs declared, "Who shall save us from Western civilization?!"

His self-described "cultural terrorism" attacked Hungary's Christian mores on sex by developing an anything-goes sex education curriculum in Hungarian schools. Unfortunately for Lukacs, Hungary's Marxist government fell when workers and traditionalists refused to support Lenin's Soviet puppet dictator Bela Kun and Lukacs' offensive cultural terrorism. Lukacs fled Hungary and connected with Gramsci in Vienna, Austria, where they exchanged ideas on how to further stealth cultural Marxism. In 1923, Lukacs teamed up with the son of a millionaire, Felix Weil, in Germany, where their "Marxist Work Week" led to the establishment of a think tank at Frankfurt University called the Institute for Marxism.

Realizing that the title for the Institute was not too stealthy, they changed it to the Institute for Social Research, and eventually it became known as the Frankfurt School, which was modeled after the Marx-Engels Institute in Moscow. Many of the Frankfurt School "thinkers" were Jews who, as atheists, rejected biblical Judaism. By 1933, realizing that National Socialism or Nazism had no room for their brand of socialism and their Jewish blood, they fled to America whose Judeo-Christian culture ironically and hypocritically they despised, and whose republican form of government under God they detested.

Having more freedom than ever before, they landed university teaching jobs throughout the United States from Columbia, New York, to the University of Wisconsin-Madison and the University of California-Berkeley. With covert calculation they set about to disseminate and indoctrinate young impressionable minds throughout the '30s, '40s, '50s, and the Revolutionary '60s with "Critical Theory."

Mixing cultural Marxism with the then-popular, sexually debased Freudian psychoanalysis, Critical Theory was the destructive criticism and denigration of the main elements of western civilization:

> Christianity, authority, the family, patriarchy, traditional values, patriotism, sexual restraint, and American republicanism.

With unrelenting criticism of every traditional and Christian institution, especially the family, the cultural Marxists hoped to not only wear down their opponents but to have them eventually join the cause. Max Horkheimer's Freudian-Marxian mix did not agree with Karl Marx's emphasis on the oppression of the worker by the rich, but taught that mankind was in a constant state of psychological repression by Christian civilization which perpetuated a monogamous, "husband and wife culture" at the expense and oppression of homosexuals and other "natural" sexual lifestyles. Horkheimer's colleague Theodor Adorno, wrote in 1950 the book *The Authoritarian Personality*, with a since proven bogus "F-scale." In the book, he concluded that the traditional patriarchal family whose mores in many cases derived from the Christian culture was "F" or Fascist. Adorno concluded that men were fascist towards women. White men were fascist towards minorities and it was fascist to not accept alternative sexual lifestyles such as homosexuality. It is not a coincidence that on college campuses today the common term used by the Left for people who disagree with their worldview is fascist. Evolving out of this thinking was the view that history was determined by which group had power or dominance over other groups. White males became the main oppressors in society while minorities were always the victims.

Minorities were automatically good and oppressed while white male Christians were automatically bad. Individual character and behavior no longer mattered but group identification did. The Jewish-German-born philosopher-writer Herbert Marcuse wrote *Eros and Civilization* in 1955. In typical Frankfurt School style, Marcuse's *Eros* is a synthesis of the atheist Jews Karl Marx and Sigmund Freud who rejected Judaism and Judaism's child, Christianity. As an atheist Jew who rejected Judaism, Marcuse argued that mankind needed to "liberate non-procreative eros" through "polymorphous perversity." In other words, people are free to engage in "perversions" in defiance of the enslavement of Christian morality and capitalism. Marcuse argued that by freeing sex from any moral restraints, we could elevate the pleasure principle over the reality principle and create a playful society with no work. Such defiance and playfulness will, as in other cultural-Marxian practices, wear down their opponents, eventually seeing many joining their ranks.

Marcuse took from Freud's psychology the technique of psychological conditioning. While Marcuse believed that there was a time and place to argue a point philosophically, in many cases to "normalize" behavior considered "abnormal" or "sinful" in Christian culture, one should infuse the culture with counterculture values and images. For example, with homosexuality, society should be conditioned over time with magazines, movies, and television show after television show projected into every American home where the only normal-seeming white male is a homosexual, and the "new-normal" family is Adam and Steve or Ellen and Eve. What was suggested in the '50s and '60s by Marcuse has become the politically correct norm in American society where the book of Genesis' Adam and Eve are maligned and ridiculed. When Vladimir Lenin said, "of all the mediums cinema is the most important," he understood the power movies had in "normalizing" deviant behavior and stigmatizing Christian culture. Therefore, many of the Frankfurt School's key people spent their World War II years in Hollywood learning how to utilize that medium for their ultimate goal of de-Christianizing America.

With a philosophy of defiance against oppressive Christian social structures and advocacy of "playful lifestyles," Herbert Marcuse became the perfect "guru" of the '60s' drugs, sex, and rock-n-roll counterculture as his eroticized Marxism fed their sexual revolution perfectly as Marcuse's "make love not war" maxim became the mantra of the Left. During the many riots in America and Europe in the bloody revolutionary year of 1968, militant Marxist revolutionaries proudly carried signs reading, "Marx, Mao, Marcuse." Patrick Buchanan, in his excellent book, *The Death of The West*, writes of Marcuse:

Brandeis professor Herbert Marcuse was the pied piper of the sixties as he fostered the development of radical youth, feminists, black militants, homosexuals, the alienated, the asocial, Third World revolutionaries, all the angry voices of the persecuted "victims" of the West.

In 1965, Marcuse wrote a very clever tract called "Repressive Tolerance." In his essay, Marcuse argues that "pure tolerance" favors the political right and "the tyranny of the majority." Therefore we, the Left, are to have "selective tolerance" where we tolerate all ideas in society as long as they concur with cultural Marxism. The ideas that derive from Judeo-Christian traditional values are to be rejected and not tolerated.

Freedom of speech is fine as long as your speech affirms the Marxian worldview. Marcuse, in typical Marxist form, perverts the normal use of language in Orwellian and Machiavellian fashion and distorts our Founders' understanding of the first amendment and true freedom of speech.

Sadly, we see this intolerant, Marxist-Fascist mode of operation when many Christians, conservatives, libertarians, and republicans attempt to speak on college campuses and are booed down, drummed out, shouted at, or physically attacked, many times not being allowed to finish their speeches. Let us now turn to the "sixties disciples of the Frankfurt School," among them Barack Obama's dear friends Bill Ayers and Bernardine Dohrn.

CHAPTER 8

THE SIXTIES: DAYS OF RAGE & GRANT PARK, 1968 & 2008

"We were going to bring the war home. 'Turn the imperialists' war into a civil war,' in Lenin's words. And we were going to kick ass."
-John Jacobs

"I don't regret setting bombs... I feel we didn't do enough. Everything was absolutely ideal on the day I bombed the Pentagon."
-Bill Ayers

The comedian-actor Robin Williams once quipped, "If you remember the sixties you weren't there." Well, I was there and I remember the '60s all too well, the good, the bad, and the ugly.

The good. I remember when my mother, who was called "Lovely Lady of Song" when she sang with local big bands during World War II, would sing to me as I played, "He's Got the Whole World in His Hands." I remember my first communion and as an altar boy struggling to remember the Latin Mass, and choosing the confirmation name Dominic because of the famous Singing Nun song "Dominique" that was on Ed Sullivan. My buddies laughed at the name; I thought it was cool. Still do. It means LORD. I

remember the excitement of watching Vince Lombardi, Bart
Starr, and the Green Bay Packers win five NFL titles and the first
two Super Bowls. I think I was at the Ice Bowl, too. I remember
Christmas evening of 1968 when after opening my cool presents
we sat around our old RCA black-and-white TV to watch Apollo 8
see the dark side of the moon, and then showing us Earth for the
first time in history. Earth! It was surreal and magical when the
astronauts, reflecting our Judeo-Christian heritage, read from the
book of Genesis: "In the beginning God created the heavens and
the earth." I sat watching the TV with my family in awe of America
and our "space cowboys" as they reminded us of the beauty of
creation and the glory of our Creator. Little did I know at the
time that when communist cosmonauts went into the heavens,
Nikita Khrushchev bragged that they didn't see God up there.

What a difference a cosmology can have on a culture.

America's Republic under God presupposes God, His glory,
and the origin of our life and liberty.

Communist-Socialist cosmology presupposes that man is mud
with no Maker and that he is subject to its god, the State. Did
not the first Roman Catholic President John Kennedy tell us in
his 1961 inaugural address that the "rights of man come not from
the generosity of the State but from the hand of God?"

The bad. I remember in my Catholic elementary school, Sacred
Heart, Sister Julius running into our classroom to dismiss us to
go home because President Kennedy had been shot. I remember

seeing my mother by our old RCA black-and-white TV crying as CBS's Walter Cronkite told us the President was dead.

The bad for my dad. My brother and I, on Sunday night, February 9, 1964, sat in our living room watching Ed Sullivan and singing with the Beatles, I Want To Hold Your Hand. I thought it was great! Little did I know that within a few years the Beatles that I so loved would be a cultural tool to weaken America's moral fiber. Let me explain:

To this day, aesthetically, I still love many of the songs from my generation. Every generation has troubadours, poet-singers, and musicians that express a searching for justice, peace, life's purpose, and mankind's destiny. From Dylan, the Beatles, Crosby, Stills, Nash, and Young—to the Moody Blues, Pink Floyd, and many others, as poets-musicians of old they reflected the good, the bad, and the ugly in society and the culture.

During my teen and young-adult years I saw many of these groups and found myself attracted to the lyrics that expressed a search for life's meaning and purpose, such as John Lennon's In My Life, reflecting on life, past memories, and important people in one's life; Paul McCartney's Yesterday expressing pain over a lost love, or his She's Leaving Home, the story about a teenage girl leaving home because mom and dad have never shown her true love; Moody Blues' Isn't Life Strange dealing with the daily struggles we all go through in life; and CSN&Y's Teach Your Children, calling on parents to love and teach their children well.

The harmonies, musical creativity, and poetic expressions were in many ways powerfully creative and wonderfully expressive.

With that being said and putting my '60s cultural biases and proclivities aside, the '60s troubadours either knowingly or unknowingly did convey and carry a cultural message that in many ways undermined traditional family values and America's Christian heritage.

In 1967, when Scott McKenzie sang the lovely song San Francisco (Be Sure To Wear Some Flowers in Your Hair) with the words, "All across the nation such a strange vibration, people in motion, there's a whole generation with a new explanation," the "new explanation" was the counterculture lifestyle of free love, free sex, free food, and free society at the expense of others, and was really the playground lifestyle Marx and Marcuse wrote about and envisioned in their communist paradise.

What was the counterculture countering? Christian culture.

When CSN&Y sang and practiced, "if you can't be with the one you love, love the one you're with" at Woodstock in 1969, they were simply reflecting the "commune-ism" of Marx, Marcuse, and Mao's "new communist family" which rejected Judeo-Christian monogamy, fidelity, and traditional marriage while advocating and practicing adultery, infidelity, and a myriad of alternative bohemian lifestyles and sexual practices. When Paul McCartney sang "Why don't we do it in the road" or when John Lennon wrote "Imagine," we see a fulfillment of cultural Marxism's dictum: "Through the culture without bullets we can tear down the established Christian order."

When Pink Floyd's co-founder Syd Barrett, after taking a number of acid hits, incessantly jumps up and down on his bed yelling, "I'm free! I'm free! I'm free!" he reflects the mantra of many of the '60s musicians as they wanted to be *autonomous* (Greek word for lawless) or "free" to do whatever they wanted to do with whomever they wanted to do it, with no moral restraints or God's law telling them that fornication, homosexuality, covetousness, or adultery was wrong.

Yes, all of mankind is plagued with the aforementioned sins and many more. The Judeo-Christian Scriptures tell mankind we all our sinners.

The difference is, cultural Marxism denies the fall of man and his sinful-soul condition as a natural part of his human nature. While Judaism and Christianity view man as made in the image of God, they equally concur that humanity is plagued and polluted from sin. The counterculture of the sixties was in many ways a natural conduit and fit for cultural Marxism as the hippies, yippies, communes, rock 'n rollers, poet-musicians, students, professors, and radical revolutionaries justified and defended in their music, poetry, classrooms, lifestyles, and militancy their wild and sinful ways.

Hypocrisy has plagued mankind since the Garden of Eden. At Woodstock, CSN&Y sang of getting back to the "garden," an allusion to the Garden of Eden, but their Eden, like Karl Marx's earthly Eden, was one without the God of Israel, the God of the Judeo-Christian Scriptures, or to quote the Declaration of Independence, "the Supreme Judge of the world." They did not want to be accountable to any "judgmental" God for their free love, sex, drugs, and playful, no-work lifestyle, as "that would be a bad trip, man." The counterculture trip was a trip far away from the Christian culture our Founders knew to be an essential ingredient for a successful republic. As a socialist, while John Lennon sang of imagining no possessions or of being a working-class hero, he made millions of dollars off a free-enterprise system to perpetuate his bourgeois lifestyle in America. Few people know of the two versions of his Beatles song Revolution where he says you can "count him in" on the Marxist revolution. Few people have read Lennon's 1971 interview with the communist underground newspaper The Red Mole where he discusses the infiltration of the British army and the use of Marxist ideas to change the world. As Pink Floyd's Roger Waters soaked in his father's communist worldview, advocating socialism and denigrating Christianity in his songs like Time, where he calls the gospel the "softly spoken magic spell," he became a millionaire a hundred times over within a capitalistic system he spent a lifetime attacking.

Yes, I do have an affinity to troubadours, to creative forces within a society that think outside the box and help us see life in different categories. However, while I am attracted to various creative art forms aesthetically, I have come to see that troubadours can be used, to quote Gramsci, to "change the established culture." Musicians, poets, and actors have traditionally gravitated to the left wing of the political spectrum throughout history. It is there that they have a natural home that fits their searching and dreaming ways of finding freedom without judgment. By nature, these countercultural town criers seek a newer world, a peaceful world, a playful world, and a just world. The left-wing worldview theoretically gives them the answer that jives with their vision of a heavenly experience here on the earth without the moral restraints of the Kingdom of Heaven.

Almost all of the sixties troubadours were participants in the left-wing politics of the day, with an affinity towards various social-istic, communistic movements. As the Beatles, Pink Floyd, Rolling Stones, CSN&Y, Bob Dylan, and many, many more rejected the Judeo-Christian worldview and conservative family values, they readily contributed their voices to the counterculture radicalism of their generation. One of the many musical countercultural examples would be the Rolling Stone magazine, which since its inception in 1970 with John Lennon on its first cover, has been a spokesperson for the Radical Left and an avid critic of Christianity and the Conservative Right. Even in the year 2011, Rolling Stone sided with the communist Occupy Wall Street crowd and attacked Christian family values, the Tea Party, conservatives, libertarians, and Republicans.

There is nothing new under the sun when it comes to com-munist culture and musicians of years gone by. In the '30s, '40s, and '50s, famous folk singers like Pete Seeger, Woody Guthrie, and the Almanac singers out of Greenwich Village joined the Popular Front, an alliance of liberals, hard-core leftists, and the Communist Party USA whose slogan, under their leader Earl Browder, was "Communism is twentieth-century Americanism."

Pete Seeger and Woody Guthrie, icons of the '60s folk-rock era, like Bob Dylan and Bruce Springsteen, sang songs glorifying communism, socialism, and Joseph Stalin. Woody Guthrie, the "Dust Bowl troubadour," whose guitar displayed in big letters, "This Machine Kills Fascists," so hated the song God Bless America that he wrote the song This Land Is Your Land to reflect his communist worldview. How stupid and foolish they looked when Soviet Socialist "St. Stalin" joined murderous National Socialist fascist Hitler to rape, pillage, and murder millions of Europeans in the beginning of World War II.

With their affinity towards the world of Karl Marx, you'd never see "This Machine Kills Communists" on the guitars of the folk and rock musicians of the '50s and '60s. Unfortunately, that same naive, double standard is alive today in the world of rock. Incidentally, Pete Seeger, age 93 now, is still alive and joined with rock 'n roller Bruce Springsteen and Crosby, Stills, Nash, and Young to campaign in 2008 for Senator Obama while attacking conservative Christian values.

As things change, things remain the same.

The same goes for Hollywood. Vladimir Lenin's famous quote, "Of all the arts, for us the most important is cinema," explains why he and Joseph Stalin infiltrated the conservative Hollywood establishment with "useful idiots" to hopefully take over the film industry. Coinciding with the Popular Front, the Soviet Comintern, using Fabian tactics and strategies, created "innocent clubs and organizations" in order to infiltrate the culture with Marxist ideas. The Comintern's goal was to:

> Penetrate every conceivable milieu, get hold of artists and professors, make use of cinemas and theatres, and spread abroad the doctrine that Russia is prepared to sacrifice everything to keep the world at peace. We must join these clubs ourselves.

Daniel Flynn, in his book *A Conservative History of the American Left*, writes:

> The multitude of "innocent clubs" which American Communists started and not just infiltrated, the New Theater League, the Hollywood Anti-Nazi League, the New Dance League, and the League of American Writers. This last group managed to sign up Franklin Roosevelt, demonstrating how deep into the mainstream Soviet fronts penetrated.

Flynn goes on to say, "The 1930s was the decade when smart people acted stupid" Not only did they act stupid, but they held a double standard when it came to choosing anti-totalitarianism. They had no problem having a "Hollywood Anti-Nazi League" but they would never have dreamed of creating a "Hollywood Anti-Commie League." Pete Seeger and Woody Guthrie's "fascist killing machine" mindset was duplicated when a significant number of

Hollywood writers, directors, and producers became comrades as "communist cultural warriors," conveying in their cinema the glory of Stalin's Socialism. Like the embarrassed Pete Seeger and Woody Guthrie, when "St. Stalin" joined Fascist-Socialist Hitler to butcher Poland and Eastern Europe in 1939, there was silence on the Hollywood left front.

A mythology has been perpetuated by lefty historians and Hollywood writers that a fascist witch hunt and burning occurred in the 1940s and 1950s in America by Republicans and conservative Democrats. Michael Berliner of *Capitalist* magazine writes:

> **Lie Number One:** By requiring them to testify and then jailing them for refusing, the House Un-American Activities Committee violated the First Amendment, free-speech rights of the Hollywood Ten.
>
> **The truth:** No one interfered with their freedom of speech. In fact, freedom of speech was not even an issue. HUAC was investigating a question of fact, the fact being membership in the Communist Party. The Committee did not ask anyone whether he believed in communism, but asked only whether he had joined the Communist Party. By joining the Party (an undisputed fact), the filmmakers were not merely making an ideological statement but were agreeing to take orders to commit actions—criminal and treasonable actions, since the Party, and the Soviet government it served, was openly dedicated to the overthrow of the U.S. government. Therefore, there was a national security reason for the Committee to determine membership in the Party.

Lie Number Two: The Hollywood Ten were persecuted by being refused jobs.

The truth: They were denied employment by executives who were exercising the right to hire whom they wished—a fundamental right in a free society. It was within the employers' right (and self-interest) not to hire writers who wanted to use their positions to eliminate all private property and private business. In a free society, there is a private right to boycott (which the Hollywood leftists used against hundreds of anti-Communists). The right to freedom of speech prohibits the government from interfering with the expression of ideas, and that means that an employer cannot be forced to propagate ideas he's opposed to.

Lie Number Three (the biggest lie): The blacklisted writers were humanitarian idealists.

The truth: Their "ideal" was the sacrifice of the individual to the collective, a moral viewpoint endorsed by Marxism and put into practice by the Soviet government.

It is important to note that while a significant number of Hollywood workers bought into the Marxist lies, many did not. The Motion Picture Alliance for the Preservation of American Ideals (MPAPAI) was an organization of high-profile, politically conservative members of the Hollywood film industry. It was formed in 1944 for the purpose of defending the film industry and America against communist infiltration. Members included Walt Disney, Gary Cooper, Clark Cable, Robert Taylor, John Wayne, Elia Kazan, and of course the great anti-communist warrior and president of the Screen Actors Guild, Ronald Reagan. Reagan, who voted for FDR four times, left the Democratic Party when he saw them absorb much of the left-wing, big-government socialist agenda. Reagan would not let the American Marxist-Fabians fool him into buying their lies or advocating their cause. Reagan knew that the FACT was, there were many communists in Hollywood during FDR's, Truman's, and Eisenhower's administrations.

The Soviet Union is dead, but Hollywood's lefty-liberal agenda lives on as their scripts and movies represent in many cases a culture that is anti-capitalist, anti-Christian, anti-family, anti-conservative, and anti-republican. Just ask Barbara Streisand, Oliver Stone, Susan Sarandon, Sean Penn, Danny Glover, Alec Baldwin, Matt Damon, Ed Asner, and many more who love Castro, Chavez, and Che and join forces with Radical Left-Wing causes.

Now you may say, "Whoa, wait a minute here, Dr. Jacobs. Didn't you say that cultural Marxism was a stealth, nonviolent form of Marxism? You included radical revolutionaries and militants with the counterculture!"

That is true and for a very good reason.

Remember that the ultimate goal of Marxism-Socialism, whether it is expressed in the *Communist Manifesto*, Fabian philosophy, the Frankfurt School, Gramsci's *Prison Notebooks*, or Students for a Democratic Society, is to create a New Man, a New Family, a New Society.

That New Society, whether it is achieved through militant or stealth means, is always in contradistinction to the worldview philosophy of Christianity, western civilization, and our Republic under God. In many cases, as explained before, revolutionary Marxist militants will join arm and arm in solidarity with their peaceful cultural comrades, knowing that in numbers is power and in power is the mob and in the mob is people power or democracy, also called mobocracy.

That is why many of the well-intentioned '60s students who joined SDS (Students for a Democratic Society) were shocked when SDS evolved into the Communist-Terrorist Weathermen or Weather Underground. It is not by accident that the SDS chose the word democratic for their new society: Students for a Democratic Society. They certainly would not have created the SRS, Students for a Republican Society, as that would fly in the face of their emerging worldview, which was anti-republican and pro-Marxist. While many young and unsuspecting college kids joined SDS to change the world and rearrange society, its leadership knew what they were about. I quote extensively from the book hated by the Left, *A Patriot's History of the United States*:

> It was radical students who led the attack. Many of the agitators' leaders were "red diaper babies" whose parents were Communist Party members or socialists... Tom Hayden, later known for his famous marriage to actress Jane Fonda, co-founded the Students for a Democratic Society in 1960 with Al Haber, a local Michigan radical. Haber received support from the socialist Student League for Industrial Democracy. Though publically anti-Soviet, they had no intention of opposing communism in word or principle. Steeped in Marxism,

both Haber and Hayden hated American capitalism and the middle-class society it produced. The committed Hayden—praised as "the next Lenin"—organized a meeting of activists in Port Huron, Michigan, in 1962, that produced the manifesto of the movement called the Port Huron Statement. The Port Huron Statement enjoined the students to seize control of the educational system from the administrators and government, that is, the taxpayers. Hoping to distance themselves from the Stalinist atrocities of the 1930s, the SDS and other radical organizations called themselves the New Left. One of the key tenets of the Port Huron philosophy was that the United States was the source of conflict and injustice in the world. Equally important, though, was the notion that "students were ideally suited to lead," and that the university was the ideal location, if not the only one, from which to launch the new radicalism.

The SDS has been glamorized as being the vanguard of freedom in the sixties and sanitized by leftist historians from its socialist and communist radicalism.

It is a well-known fact that before the creation of the Weathermen many of the leaders of SDS such as Carl Davidson, David Horowitz, Country Joe McDonald, and other red-diaper babies, proudly proclaimed a Marxist-Leninist worldview.

That brings me back to my '60s memories:

"The Bad and the Ugly."

In 1968, I cried when my childhood heroes Martin Luther King Jr. and Robert F. Kennedy were murdered. I still have the newspapers I saved from those tragic events. In 1968, I was suspended from Madison Junior High School for wearing all black and a black glove and for yelling down the hallways, "Civil rights for all! Freedom for all!" That was a good memory for me but not for my dad who grounded me for a week.

Called by many "The Year of Hate," 1968 saw assassinations and riots in over 100 American cities. Social unrest was prevalent as across the world there were attempts by radical Marxists to destroy "imperialist" capitalism.

One such violent activity was in Chicago's Grant Park, August 28, 1968. Immortalized by the Crosby, Stills, Nash, and Young song *Chicago*, the Democratic National Convention was held in Chicago, Illinois, from August 26 to August 29, 1968. Because Lyndon Johnson had announced in March that he would not run again for president, the convention needed to select a candidate to run against Richard Nixon. Vice President Hubert Humphrey was having an uphill battle to win the nomination, as many Democrats were torn between party loyalty and the war their party had created. Many anti-war democrats, anti-war demonstrators of various backgrounds, and militant elements of the socialist Students for a Democratic Society had gathered in Grant Park to protest the democratic party's Vietnam War. Over 10,000 demonstrators converged on Chicago during the first two days of the well-organized convention against the Vietnam War. By Tuesday afternoon, August 27, yippie Marxists, anarchists, Ho Chi Minh Marxists, and the socialist SDS were calling for revolution in the streets and crying "Kill the pigs!" With emotions raw, thousands of the demonstrators, many of them communists and anarchists, marched from the Chicago Coliseum to Grant Park.

Along the way, they spotted the hill of the Logan Statue at 9th and Michigan, and while yelling, "Take the hill!" they covered the brass statue of the Civil War hero and former Illinois senator with black anarchist flags, red communist flags, and the communist flags of North Vietnam. The Chicago police charged the hill, dispersing the militant Marxist demonstrators, whom they eventually pushed back across the Balbo Bridge into Grant Park. The following day, Wednesday, August 28, the radicals held a rally at the old band shell on the south end of Grant Park. After hearing that a party plank which supported peace in South Vietnam was voted down at the democratic convention, a militant demonstrator lowered the American flag and replaced it with a bloody shirt. The police attempted to disperse the mob as they were taunted with chants of "Hell no, we won't go!" "Pigs are whores!" and "Kill, kill, kill!" as militants in the mob attacked the police with rocks, sticks, and chunks of concrete. When thousands of people in the mob had reached the point of becoming a potentially violent mass, the police were ordered to clear the streets. Militants within the mob, and unfortunately peaceful protestors as well, were clubbed, sprayed with mace, and shoved into paddy wagons as the mob yelled out the now-famous chant, "The whole world's watching... the whole world's watching!" When the militants in the mob fought back, the confrontation with the Chicago police became more violent and all of it was brought into our living rooms on all three television networks. I still remember as I watched this mob on CBS with my dad, who was a survivor of the Great Depression, World War II, and a lifelong Democrat and union leader, that he said to me:

> "Damn, it's one thing to hate the war in Vietnam, but it's a whole other thing for these radicals to support our communist enemies by calling for revolution in the streets. Patrick, always beware of the mob."

While most accounts of the event are portrayed as a Nazi-like police action, left-wing historians very conveniently leave out the militant revolutionaries in the crowd and their call for violence and militant communist revolution by many that day. The following newspaper account, titled "The Chicago Scene" and dated August 28, 1968, summarizes the event properly.

> Massed across the street from the Conrad Hilton Hotel (Democratic Headquarters) in Chicago's Grant Park, were 10,000 demonstrators who were listening to intermittent harangues by would-be revolutionaries from loudspeakers.

> According to the August 30th "Chicago Tribune" "The voices on the loud speakers in the park were those of Tom Hayden, a founder of the radical Students for a Democratic Society who reduced Columbia University to a shambles last spring; David Dellinger, self-styled non-Soviet Communist, who organized the march on the Pentagon last October; and Jerry Rubin, head of the Youth International Party (a Communist Youth organization also knows as the "Yippies"). These revolutionar-

ies came to Chicago with the design of disrupting the Democratic Convention and taking over the streets."

The sheep who sat and listened to Hayden and the others carried Vietcong flags and the black flag of the Anarchists. Throughout the day, members of the mob harassed Chicago police.

That night, the mob surged forth from Grant Park and assaulted the police and National Guardsmen stationed around the Conrad Hilton Hotel. Throwing lye, carbon tetrachloride, naptha, bottles, bricks, molotov cocktails, obscenities, and saliva into police ranks, the demonstrators "blocked street intersections and tried to charge into hotels."

Notice how eyewitness author Bruce Compton writes:

The sheep who sat and listened to Hayden and the others carried Vietcong flags and the black flag of the anarchists. Throughout the day members of the mob harassed the Chicago police. That night, the mob surged forth from Grant Park and assaulted the police and National Guardsmen stationed around the Conrad Hilton Hotel.

Eight militant protestors in the Chicago Mob, the "Chicago 8"—Rennie Davis, David Dellinger, John Froines, Tom Hayden, Abbie Hoffman, Jerry Rubin, Bobby Seale, and Lee Weiner— were indicted by a grand jury on March 20, 1969, to be tried for conspiracy and other charges. They ALL had militant Marxist worldviews that called for the violent overthrow of our Republic under God.

Besides the radical Marxist "Chicago 8," there were two predominate SDS leaders who were in Grant Park in 1968 as the "whole world was watching," Bernardine Dohrn and Bill Ayers.

I've included a very illuminating 2009 NBC-Chicago interview with the so-called ex-communist terrorists Bill Ayers and Bernardine Dohrn discussing their Grant Park experiences in 1968 and 2008.

> Bill Ayers was "overflowing with happiness, relief, love" when he and his wife went to Grant Park with tens of thousands of Chicagoans to celebrate the election of President Barack Obama.
>
> Ayers and his wife, Bernardine Dohrn, spoke exclusively with NBC-Chicago's Dick Johnson about why they joined the election night celebration in the park, where 40 years before they helped stage the Days of Rage riots. The couple said they got last-minute tickets from a friend to be in Grant Park that night.
>
> "I couldn't stop crying a couple of times. I found the exact spot where I was beaten 40 years ago," Ayers said. "But I've never been in a crowd that large that wasn't edged with either anger or drunkenness or gluttony, and it was really an extraordinary feeling." Maligned as terrorists by Obama's opponents because of their activities in the late '60s, Ayers told NBC-Chicago that he and his wife condemn all forms of terrorism. They prefer labels like activist and radical—although these days, they're more likely to be called grandpa or grandma. Ayers and Dohrn said they chose to stifle reaction to the way their

activist past was dragged into the campaign rhetoric against Obama. But privately, they were as swept up in the history of the moment as all the rest who voted for him, and they believe some of what they did almost four decades earlier helped bring about Obama's election. "Without the struggles of the '60s... there would be no President Obama," Dohrn said.

I, like Bill Ayers, couldn't stop crying that election night, November 4, 2008, either, as I sat in my backyard by my fire pit on a relatively warm November night listening to Martin Luther King's "I Have a Dream Speech" over and over again.

My neighbor lady, who loves and voted for Obama, peaked over her fence and was surprised to see my tears. I didn't have the heart to tell her why in totality I was crying, but I did manage to say, "No longer can they say America is the most racist country in the world."

It was part of the reason for my tears, for I detest racism, but that was not the primary reason for my tears.

My tears were for our Republic under God.

After all the empirical, historical evidence, after all the blatant and obvious prima facie facts, after all my speeches and writings and thousands of Americans screaming from the rooftops about Barack Obama's Marxist-Socialist worldview, the majority of the American people, along with Oprah, Hollywood, the loony left, the militant left, the entitlement generation, the give-me-give-me-"I-want-my-Obama-money" crowd (the mob), and the elite media elected a stealth socialist, a cultural Marxist, a smooth, cunning, teleprompting Machiavellian politician that our Founders and George Orwell warned us about.

As I watched the November 4, 2008, election night celebration in Grant Park, I couldn't help but be dumbfounded, frustrated, and seriously concerned over my country's future. As a citizen and an American history teacher, I remembered the haunting words of George Orwell who wrote, "Who controls the past controls the future; who controls the present controls the past." When we sounded the alarm on the sordid and sundry connections Senator Obama had with radical and militant communists and socialists, we were called McCartyites, rabid right-wingers, and paranoid.

Even the aforementioned NBC interview says that Ayers and Dohrn were "maligned as terrorists by Obama's opponents." They were maligned because they actually WERE militant terrorists who called for a violent, bloody Marxist revolution to destroy our Republic under God, and they DID create a militant branch of the SDS called the Weathermen after a Bob Dylan song. Eventually going underground to avoid arrest by the FBI, they became known as Weather Underground who actually DID blow up bombs at least thirty times in an attempt to destroy the Pentagon, the U.S. State Department, the U.S. Capitol, and a large number of other government buildings throughout America. Bill Ayers summed up the organization's ideology as follows: "Kill all the rich people. Break up their cars and apartments. Bring the revolution home. Kill your parents."

The Weathermen had direct connections to Havana, Cuba, and communist Fidel Castro, and the USSR. Weathermen leaders like SDS's Mark Rudd traveled illegally to Cuba in 1968 to engage in terrorist training in Havana, where camps set up by Soviet KGB Colonel Vadim Kochergin were educating Americans in both Marxist philosophy and urban guerilla warfare.

In July of 1969 Apollo 11 landed on the moon as Neil Armstrong and Buzz Aldrin proudly planted our Republic's flag on its surface. Astronaut Aldrin, reflecting our Christian cosmology and heritage, and in the spirit of 1968's Apollo 8's reading from the book of Genesis, prayed and took communion, or the Lord's Supper, on the moon.

In contradistinction to the love of God and country, in 1969, Bill Ayers was one of the leaders of what they called the "Days of Rage." Over 300 militant Marxists created mayhem as they mobbed the streets of Chicago with arson, looting, vandalism, and vicious attacks on the police and innocent bystanders. Their ultimate goal was to destroy the United States and to create a communist paradise with them as "the enlightened rulers." Bill Ayers, Bernardine Dohrn, Linda Evans, John Jacobs, Jeff Jones, Mark Rudd, and many other comrades called for Marxist "re-education camps." In 1969, Larry Grathwohl, an Army veteran, joined Ayers' army and served as a messenger among the Weathermen's leadership. Grathwohl was also an FBI informant, and in a 1982 interview for the documentary, No Place To Hide, Grathwohl revealed what

Ayers' army was going to do after they destroyed the U.S. government, especially with those who refused to endorse communism.

> I asked, "Well, what is going to happen to those people we can't re-educate, that are diehard capitalists?" And the reply was that they'd have to be eliminated. And when I pursued this further, they estimated they would have to eliminate 25 million people in these reeducation centers. And when I say "eliminate," I mean 'kill.' Twenty-five million people. I want you to imagine sitting in a room with 25 people, most of which have graduate degrees, from Columbia and other well-known educational centers, and hear them figuring out the logistics for the elimination of 25 million people. And they were dead serious.

In 1974, Ayers and Dohrn wrote a book titled *Prairie Fire*. The title was an allusion to the biggest Marxist mass murderer in history, Mao Zedong, when in 1930 he opined that "a single spark can start a prairie fire." *Prairie Fire* was a Marxist diatribe on the evils of America's imperialist, capitalist, racist, and religious society that needed to be destroyed through militant Marxist means.

Here are a few of Ayres' and Dohrn's communist viewpoints from the book:

> We are a guerrilla organization. We are communist women and men... deeply affected by the historic events of our time in the struggle against U.S. imperialism.

> Our intention is to disrupt the empire, to incapacitate it, to put pressure on the cracks, to make it hard to carry out

its bloody functioning against the people of the world, to join the world struggle, to attack from the inside.

The only path to the final defeat of imperialism and the building of socialist is revolutionary war.

Without mass struggle there can be no revolution. Without armed struggle there can be no victory.

We need a revolutionary communist party in order to lead the struggle, give coherence and direction to the fight, seize power and build the new society.

Socialism is the total opposite of capitalism/ imperialism. It is the rejection of empire and white supremacy. Socialism is the violent overthrow of the bourgeoisie, the establishment of the dictatorship of the proletariat, and the eradication of the social system based on profit.

Revolutionary war will be complicated and protracted. It includes mass struggle and clandestine struggle, peaceful and violent, political and economic, cultural and military, where all forms are developed in harmony with the armed struggle.

Their book was dedicated to Sirhan Sirhan, the murderer of my childhood hero, Robert F. Kennedy.

I want to bring to your attention again to the last quote from the book *Prairie Fire*:

Revolutionary war will be complicated and protracted. It includes mass struggle and clandestine struggle, peaceful and violent, political and economic, cultural and military, where all forms are developed in harmony with the armed struggle.

Look at Ayers' and Dohrn's, Marx, Lenin, Stalin, Mao, Che, Castro, Fabian, Gramsci, and Frankfurt language. Their American communist revolution will be long, involving the mob; it will be clandestine or secret; it will be BOTH violent and peaceful; and it will not only include economics and the military but culture and politics.

What is the subtitle of the book you are reading?

> *The Cultural & Political War to*
> *Destroy our Republic under God.*

Ironically, on the day America was attacked by militant Muslims, September 11, 2001, so-called ex-militant Marxist Bill Ayers was interviewed by the New York Times in an article titled "No Regrets for a Love of Explosives; In a Memoir of Sorts, a War Protestor Talks of Life with the Weathermen." I have selected a few quotes and passages from the interview to show you the bizarre, lying, "revolutionary" mind:

> Now he has written a book, *Fugitive Days* (Beacon Press, September). Mr. Ayers, who is 56, calls it a memoir; somewhat coyly perhaps, since he also says some of it is fiction. He writes that he participated in the bombings of New York City police headquarters in 1970, of the Capitol building in 1971, and the Pentagon in 1972. But Mr. Ayers also seems to want to have it both ways, taking responsibility for daring acts in his youth, then deflecting it. "I don't regret setting bombs," Bill Ayers

said. "I feel we didn't do enough." So, would Mr. Ayers do it all again? he is asked. "I don't want to discount the possibility," he said.

Marxists are notorious for lying, twisting the truth, having selective memories and amnesia, perverting and inverting history, and speaking out of both sides of their mouths as they use gobbledygook and convoluted language to continue their clandestine struggle. Like the Fabian wolf in sheep's clothing, they hope to fool some of the people all of the time and all of the people some of the time. And unfortunately, as cultural Marxism, secular humanism, and progressivism permeate our education system in America today, they are close to fooling almost all the people all of the time. In fact, they are so good at fooling the people that when militant Marxists are asked why they advocated violence in various forms back in the day, they say it was a joke and many people buy that! Here are a few not-so-funny comments by Ayers and Dohrn in their infamous 9/11 New York Times interview:

Mr. Ayers, who in 1970 was said to have summed up the Weathermen philosophy as: "Kill all the rich people. Break up their cars and apartments. Bring the revolution home. Kill your parents. That's where it's really at," is today distinguished professor of education at the University of Illinois at Chicago. And he says he doesn't actually remember suggesting that rich people be killed or that people kill their parents, but "it's been quoted so many times I'm beginning to think I did," he said. "It was a joke about the distribution of wealth." In 1967, he met Ms. Dohrn in Ann Arbor, Michigan. She had a law degree from the University of Chicago and was a magnetic speaker who often wore thigh-high boots and miniskirts. In 1969, after the Manson family murders in Beverly Hills, Ms. Dohrn told an SDS audience: "Dig it! Manson killed those pigs; then they ate dinner in the same room with them; then they shoved a fork into a victim's stomach." In Chicago recently, Ms. Dohrn said of her remarks: "It was a joke. We were mocking violence in America. Even in my most inflamed moment I never supported a racist mass murderer."

I have taken time and space to describe the Students for a Democratic Society, Ayers' army, the Weather Underground, and the revolutionary Days of Rage in the '60s because there is a two-fold importance that is relevant for us today: cultural Marxism and Barack Obama.

There WAS an attempt by militant Marxists in the '60s to destroy our Republic under God. Fortunately for freedom it failed. Unfortunately, many in Ayers' army, after going underground in the '70s, came above ground and changed tactics and strategies by teaching at major established educational institutions in America such as Colombia University, New York University, the University of Chicago-Illinois, the University of Michigan, the University of Wisconsin-Madison, the University of California-Berkley, and hundreds of other universities and colleges across this great land. Fulfilling Antonio Gramsci's vision of infiltrating Christian society, Ayers and his Marxist-cultural comrades have joined ranks in the halls of academia with the disciples of the Frankfurt Marxist

School. These born-again "pacifist" Marxists became teachers of America's future teachers who for the last forty years have been teaching our children from kindergarten to college. Before we cover Marxist-terrorist Professor Bill Ayers' "conversion" to Fabian cultural Marxism, we need to cover the educational Marxist legacy the '60s gave America's children.

CHAPTER 9

WE WON THE TEXTBOOKS!

"How do you tell a communist? Well, it's someone who reads Marx and Lenin. And how do you tell an anti-Communist? It's someone who understands Marx and Lenin."
-Ronald Reagan

"Give me four years to teach the children and the seed I have sown will never be uprooted." – "Give us the child for 8 years and it will be a Bolshevik forever."
-Vladimir Lenin

"Every child in America entering school at the age of five is mentally ill because he comes to school with certain allegiances to our Founding Fathers, toward our elected officials, toward his parents, toward a belief in a supernatural being."
-Professor Chester M. Pierce, M.D., Professor Of Education And Psychiatry At Harvard

A fellow comrade of Bill Ayers is Todd Gitlin, president of SDS in 1965, and today he is a professor of sociology at Columbia University. As Professor Gitlin reflects on Reagan becoming governor of California in 1966, and Nixon winning the White House in 1968, he candidly states:

My generation of the New Left—a generation that grew as the [Vietnam] war went on—relinquished any title to patriotism without much sense of loss. All that was left to the Left was to unearth righteous traditions and cultivate them in universities. The much-mocked political correctness of the next academic generations was a consolation prize. We lost—we squandered the politics—but won the textbooks.

"We... won the textbooks."

The radical-socialist-communist left WON the textbooks! I want you to think of the ramifications of the statement.

The textbooks!

One of the major tools used by teachers to shape the worldview, the mindset, and the thinking of young impressionable minds are textbooks. Sadly, New-Left Professor Todd Gitlin is spot-on!

What does this mean for our republic today?

If it continues it means a disaster.

The preface to Sandra Stotsky's report, "The Stealth Curriculum: Manipulating America's History Teachers," states:

> If American teachers of history were broadly educated and deeply knowledgeable about the subjects for which they're responsible in the classroom, and if they were free to draw their information, textbooks, and other instructional materials from whatever sources they judge best, all within a framework of sound academic standards and results-based accountability—under that dreamy set of circumstances, this report would not be necessary. The sad reality, however, is that many of our history teachers don't know enough history. To make matters worse, the textbooks on which they typically depend are

vast yet surprisingly shabby compendia of dull, dated, and denatured information.

Professor Stotsky shares her concerns over the survival of our republic due to poorly trained teachers when she writes:

> We need to address as soon as possible the serious threat to the American experiment in self-government posed by the growing use of anti-civic and anti-intellectual curriculum materials by academically weak history or social studies teachers who have not been trained to think critically about what they are given to use.

"The Stealth Curriculum: Manipulating America's History Teachers" draws some alarming conclusions that confirm my experiences in public school education for three decades. Many teachers are poorly trained, academically weak, have not been taught how to think critically, and are not free to choose a curriculum that is *politically incorrect*. Not only have many of them been indoctrinated with a left-wing, anti-civic, and anti-intellectual curriculum, they have, whether due to their biases, naivety, or politically correct pressure, perpetuated an anti-civic, anti-intellectual curriculum. We must liberate the textbooks, the classrooms, the teachers, and our children from the chains of politically correct cultural Marxism. It is imperative for our young people to feed at the fountain of the wisdom of our Founding Founders. In his eighth annual address to Congress on December 7, 1796, President George Washington, in stressing education for our nation, wisely stated:

A primary object should be the education of our youth in the science of government. In a republic, what species of knowledge can be equally important? And what duty more pressing than communicating it to those who are to be the future guardians of the liberties of the country?

That is the KEY to unlock the chains of communistic control over the education of our youth! To save our Republic under God the teaching of the republican science of government to our youth is our last hope.

How did we drift so far away from our godly republican roots?

By and large we ignored the infiltration, permeation, and saturation of our Christian culture with an alternative worldview that has now filled the minds of millions in America with Marx's madness, and has created a counterculture whose tentacles have wrapped themselves around a number of our influential institutions.

This is why Barack Obama's past with radical communist-socialist educators, terrorists, politicians, and community organizers in "Red Chicago" made very little impact among the American people in 2008! Should we be surprised when many of our young people, teachers, and citizens get their understanding of the news from comedian Jon Stewart or New Age talk-show host Oprah Winfrey? As you know, I cried for my country when Obama was elected in 2008, knowing that as an American history teacher I didn't do enough to stop this Fabian onslaught.

Obama advisor socialist Princeton Professor Cornell West states: "Marxist thought becomes even more relevant after the collapse of communism in the Soviet Union and Eastern Europe than it was before." As I have written earlier, even though we won the Cold War of militant Marxism, we are losing the war of Marxist thought, of creeping socialism, and of disguised cultural Marxism. I believe that many of the battles we have lost in this cultural war have been lost in the classroom because government schools since the '60s have overwhelmingly presented a politically correct one-sided, biased viewpoint of American history. It was Karl Marx who said that one of the first battles for communists to wage was to rewrite history, and rewrite history is exactly what many of America's left-wing professors of history have done.

Due to the influences of Gramsci, the Fabians, the Frankfurt School, and progressive educators, this new left-wing history sees America as a dark, oppressive land where minorities, women, homosexuals, atheists, secularists, Muslims, and all religions except Judaism and Christianity are constantly being discriminated against and vilified by conservative, Christian, Republican white males. This rewritten history emphasizes "the bad and the ugly" in America and downplays "the good and the great" in our history. This imbalanced history denigrates our Founders as antiquated, authoritarian, imperialistic, racist white men. They write, preach, and teach more on Indian massacres, slavery, Japanese internment camps, and bombs on Hiroshima and Nagasaki than about the events that ended the slavery of National Socialism, Soviet Socialism, and Japanese Imperialism (i.e., D-Day, Iwo Jima, Anzio, and the Cold War). While pointing out all of America's foibles, sins, and degradations, they rarely if ever discuss the fact that millions of oppressed people from around the world are literally dying to come here for opportunities of economic prosperity, social mobility, and freedom! This distorted history cries out with Jesse Jackson, "Hey, hey, ho, ho, western civs got to go!" as college curricula in the last forty years has denigrated western civilization, Christianity, our Founders, and republicanism while venerating multiculturalism, African studies, feminist studies, and lesbian, gay, bisexual, and transvestite studies.

In 1963, as communism grew bolder in our culture, we were warned by a few brave souls of the covert designs of communism. Democratic congressman from Florida A. S. Herlong spoke before Congress on January 10, 1963, on communism's forty-five goals to overtake America. Goal number seventeen is relevant to American culture, education, and textbooks as it reads:

> 17. Get control of the schools. Use them as transmission belts for socialism and current Communist propaganda. Soften the curriculum. Get control of teachers' associations. Put the party line in textbooks.

The forty-four other communist goals would take another book, but number seventeen is profound enough!

I'm not saying that all high school and college teachers are communists—far from it—or that the National Education Association is explicitly communist or that the Democratic Party is a communist party. But...

There are large numbers of people within American government schools, teachers' unions, and the Democratic Party with an affinity towards cultural Marxism, as cultural Marxists utilize the clever bogus language of democracy and social justice to fool the untrained or unsuspecting eye. While many of my colleagues at the Madison, Wisconsin, social studies conventions were not explicit advocates of Marxism, they were "anti-anti-communists" whose liberal Democratic Party big-government worldview gave them an affinity to watered-down communism or "compassionate communism" without the violence. Many of them never understood my equal hatred for communism and Nazism. While Nazism called for race warfare, communism called for class warfare. While Nazism murdered over twenty million, communism murdered well over 100 million. They also never understood my equal hatred for the socialist red-flagged hammer and sickle as the socialist red-flagged swastika.

When Hollywood lefty Matt Damon plugs his neighbor and professor friend Howard Zinn's book *A People's History of the United States* in the film *Good Will Hunting*, most in the audience do not know that Zinn's book, one of the most popular history textbooks at both the high school and college levels in America, is a Marxist tome that detests our Republic under God. In discussing the founding of America, Professor Zinn writes:

> Around 1776 certain important people in the English colonies made a discovery that would prove enormously useful for the next two hundred years. They found that by creating a nation, a symbol, a legal unity called the United States, they could take over land, profits, and political power from the favorites of the British Empire.

In the process, they could hold back a number of potential rebellions and create a consensus of popular support for the rule of a new, privileged leadership.

In Howard Zinn's Marxist academic world, America's Founders are all about the pursuit of exploitation and profit at the expense of the people by feigning a democratic rhetoric of life, liberty, and the pursuit of happiness. Zinn goes on to say:

> When we look at the American Revolution this way, it was a work of genius, and the Founding Fathers deserve the awed tribute they have received over the centuries. They created the most effective system of national control devised in modern times, and showed future generations of leaders the advantages of combining paternalism with command.

July 4, 1776, to Zinn is not one the great seminal events in world history for the advancement of life and liberty, but is portrayed as a controlling totalitarian tragedy. Zinn is so far left that in his book, *A People's History of the United States*, he criticizes FDR's New Deal for not going far enough to redistribute wealth in the U.S. during the Great Depression. Zinn argues that FDR was primarily concerned with saving American capitalism, and that he should have been more radical in nationalizing American industry and promoting economic socialism. In classic Marxian language Zinn says of his goal as a writer and teacher of history:

> I wanted my writing of history and my teaching of history to be a part of a social struggle... I wanted to be a

part of history and not just a recorder and teacher of history. So that kind of attitude towards history, history itself as a political act, has always informed my writing and my teaching.

When Howard Zinn's Marxist theory clashes with historical facts, Karl Marx wins every time. Zinn's "political act" was to be a "master of cheap Marxist propaganda" and not a true historian. A *People's History of the United States* is a twisted history that is anti-capitalistic, anti-Christian, and anti-republic, designed to fit his socialistic aims. Hypocritically, as Zinn attacks capitalism and the country that protected his freedom to be foolish, his Marxist books made him a millionaire.

History Professor Paul Kengor writes:

> The leftist intelligentsia that dominates higher education, and which writes the civics texts used in high schools— I've read and studied these texts—and which trains the teachers who teach in high schools, is not in the slightest bit notably anti-communist. These liberals do not teach the lessons of communism.

While there is a heavy emphasis in our high schools and colleges on the evils of National Socialism (Nazism) and rightfully so, there is a negligence or imbalance in teaching on the vile, bloody, evil history of communism's variants: Soviet Socialism, Chinese Socialism, Cuban Socialism, Korean Socialism, et al. In the twenty-plus years I attended social studies conventions in Madison, Wisconsin, there were wonderful presentations on

Hitler, the Holocaust, Fascism, and Nazism, but rarely, if ever, presentations on the evils of Lenin, Stalin, Mao, Castro, and Che. In fact, many of the history colleagues I dialogued with justified the Marxist-Bolsheviks' mass murder, downplayed Stalin's "Holocaust" in the Ukraine, and were fans of Fidel Castro and Che Guevara. As Professor Paul Kengor states:

> Being on the left entails many strange contradictions and political pathologies, one of which is this bizarre revulsion toward anti-communists. These leftists—to their credit—despise fascism, and will preach anti-fascism until they're blue in the face. They are as appalled by fascism as conservatives are by communism. But while conservatives detest both communism and fascism, liberals only detest one of the two.

In my many years of high school and college history teaching, I have noticed how conservatives and leftists despise Hitler's *Mein Kampf* while many leftists love Marx's *The Communist Manifesto*.

Both would never use Hitler's book as a tool for social insight, while many leftist professors quote profusely from Marx's *Manifesto* and require it for not just historical reading but as a tool of teaching social justice. Conservatives consider *The Communist Manifesto* one of the most evil books ever written, developing the worldview that fed the ideas, thinking, and actions behind communism's bloody reign of terror that killed over 100 million. Throughout my career I have seen a number of high school and college instructors defend Che Guevara and the students who wear T-shirts adorning his image. I have had students of mine wear Che T-shirts and Mao

Zedong patches on their purses or jeans and nobody bats an eye. Wear a Hitler T-shirt or jeans patch and watch the condemnation.

That is why when I visit the University of Wisconsin-Madison and go into many of the shops on State Street, I am not surprised to see them filled with T-shirts, coffee cups, and posters glorifying the heroes of communism, but none with T-shirts and coffee cups of Adolf Hitler or Adolf Eichmann. Once in a while when I go to my state capital and visit these lefty shops, while carrying one of their Che or Mao coffee cups, I ask them if they have any Hitler or Mussolini cups and the usual response with incredulity is:

"Now why would I sell cups of fascist murderers in my shop?"

My usual response with counter-incredulity is: "Considering you're selling the cups of communist mass murderers—a philosophy that destroyed freedom of religion, speech, press, private property, the right to own your own shop, and was responsible for the death of over 100 million people in the twentieth century, I thought you'd like to give equal sales opportunity to Nazis and fascists!"

These paraphernalia shops, which have every New Age, secular, socialist, communist, anti-conservative, and anti-Christian item available, are very popular in college towns, as they reflect what many young adults in America are learning in their political science, history, literature, ethnic studies, gay studies, sociology, and psychology courses. Instead of their education being truly progressive, it is in reality regressive, oppressive, and anti-republican.

Jake Jacobs with President Ronald Reagan - 1998

CHAPTER 10

THE PROGRESSIVES AND BIGGER GOVERNMENT

> "Father, there are many who want to destroy us from outside this nation, folks like al-Qaeda and the radical Islamists. But there are folks that want to destroy us from inside, the progressives and the socialists, who want to make this nation a nation that's no longer under you, under God, but a nation that's ruled by man."
> -U.S. Rep. Paul Broun (R-Athens)

In his 2006 book *Cultural Warrior*, Bill O'Reilly creates an imaginary 2020 State of the Union speech from an imaginary hard-core, left-wing progressive president, Gloria Hernandez. Here are a few excerpts from President Hernandez's speech:

> My fellow Americans... We are well on our way to completing our program of making America a more just, progressive society based upon-secular humanism!... We will be able to live our lives as true individuals, without moral limitations imposed by theocrats and others who seeks to regulate legal private conduct... We have begun a system of progressive taxation-assets, not just income that will redistribute wealth from the very few to the many... The New Progressive Initiative (PIT) that caps America's net worth at $15 million... my

fellow Americans, perhaps most important, America is leading the way on championing the rights of children... each student will be free to choose his or her own curriculum... my doctrine of personal happiness for all Americans, including children, is a cornerstone of the secular-progressive movement. As you know the Supreme Court has ruled that religious expression is to be prohibited in the public square... Thus, the words "In God We Trust" are no longer on the United States currency. Our secular-progressive, one-world vision will triumph over the doubters and evildoers, of that I am sure. Finally, to those who disagree with the progressive vision that has taken root in America, I reach out and hope you will join us. There is no place in this country for greed, bias, judgmental behavior, aggression, religious zealotry, or exclusionary policies... For far too long, traditionalists, conservatives, and other misguided Americans have encouraged division by religious and economic philosophies that lead to exclusion and suffering and income inequality. Those anti-progressive forces are still among us but they are rapidly losing influence to the enlightened followers of secular humanism. The new world has indeed arrived...

God forbid that a president like Bill O'Reilly's imaginary Hernandez ever becomes president of our Republic under God.

Wait! O'Reilly's book was published in 2006 and probably written in 2005. That is well before anyone heard of the progressive, hard-core, Marxist-educated, socialist senator from Illinois,

Barack Hussein Obama. Before Obama stood on the national stage, Bill O'Reilly very perceptively states this in *Cultural Warrior*:

> No politician today would dare state this secular-progressive program openly, because the country is not ready for this agenda. But believe me: The vision articulated by President Hernandez is on the drawing board. The armies of secularism are rising and the public is largely unaware of what is taking place.

Stop! Re-read O'Reilly's statement.

He could have not been more right on even if he had a future reading machine. He described to a tee Barack Hussein Obama! Soldiers of socialism, companies of communism, and platoons of progressivism or "armies of secularism" have penetrated American culture and politics in alarming numbers. In a discussion of presidential election 2008 with a progressive atheist friend of mine from England, Barack Obama's "religious" background was brought up. This friend asked if I thought an atheist could ever be elected president of the United States. I said not now but we are heading in that direction. Obama in classic Machiavellian, manipulative form choreographed his "religious" background in Chicago to obtain political power. He attended a racist mega church with left-wing political connections whose pastor hates Jews and most whites and teaches and preaches Marxist-Black Liberation theology. Obama has used religious rhetoric to pander and appease the religious Left and the Right. He has ridiculed the Scriptures, as pointed out by Dr. James Dobson, and in many cases Obama begrudgingly upholds America Judeo-Christian traditions for his American audience.

While many pundits and I warned Americans in 2008 of Obama's communist education, stealth socialism, anti-Christian worldview, and progressive agenda, Americans still elected as president THE most hard-core, left-wing candidate in the Senate.

With the imprimatur of New Age Queen Oprah, lefty Hollywood stars, rock-n-rollers, the elite media, university professors, impressionable college kids, and sundry communist, socialist, anarchist, secular humanist, and progressive groups, along with the fanatical endorsement of Rolling Stone magazine's anointed messiah on its cover, Barack Hussein Obama was elected president of the United States.

Twelve years before Bill O'Reilly's imaginary President Hernandez.

The cultural and political war to destroy our Republic under God in 2012 is NOW more than ever at a critical survival stage!

Before I highlight President Obama's often-ignored but obvious hard-core cultural and political connections, we need to explain why those of us concerned with the death of our republic connect "progressives" with Obama and his anti-American allies—the socialists, communists, and secular humanists.

A brief history of progressivism is needed.

Many in the Democratic Party and on the Left today call themselves "progressive" because of their comradeship with the principals and worldview of America's original progressives dating from the late 1800s to the end of World War I. Contrasting with the limited republican government worldview of America's Founders, progressives were passionate advocates of ever-expanding big governmental social policies to theoretically solve America's social woes. While many conservatives today point to FDR's New Deal with big government and the welfare state as the start of what we have today, it was FDR who invoked the progressive ideas of Teddy Roosevelt and Woodrow Wilson in his 1932 campaign. While rejecting the radical revolutionary ideas of the communists and socialists, progressives like Roosevelt and Wilson had a kinship with their big-state, anti-Founding Fathers' viewpoints. In his 1887 essay titled "Socialism and Democracy," Woodrow Wilson states that he had no problem with socialism's advocacy of unfettered state power over individual rights, and "that no line can be drawn between private and public affairs which the State may not cross at will." Wilson writes that socialism's big-government viewpoint was merely the logical extension of genuine democratic theory which gives all the power to the people who can, in turn, collectively through government force eliminate undemocratic ideas like the rights of the individual.

He states again in his "Socialism and Democracy":

> In fundamental theory socialism and democracy are almost if not quite one and the same. They both rest at bottom upon the absolute right of the community to determine its own destiny and that of its members. Limits of wisdom and convenience to the public control

there may be; limits of principle there are, upon strict analysis, none.

In like manner, progressive Teddy Roosevelt argued for an ever-growing State that had the power to override individual rights of private property that slowed or stopped the progressive desire to see government-sanctioned approval of the property's social usefulness. He wrote:

> We grudge no man a fortune in civil life if it is honorably obtained and well used. It is not even enough that it should have been gained without doing damage to the community. We should permit it to be gained only so long as the gaining represents benefit to the community. This, I know, implies a policy of a far more active governmental interference with social and economic conditions in this country than we have yet had, but I think we have got to face the fact that such an increase in governmental control is now necessary.

It is important to note that while progressives, communists, and socialists had similar viewpoints when it came to their conviction that America's government must be much bigger to solve our social ills, they were not militant-Marxist monsters like the communists and socialists of their day, although unfortunately many progressives did buy into the idiotic pseudoscience of eugenics or genocidal racism. Earlier we discussed the Socialist Party of America's presidential candidate Eugene Debs who ran against Roosevelt and Wilson in 1912. In that campaign the three shared a big-government philosophy but not Debs' communist militancy.

Their "progressive militancy" was to come in the form of anti-constitutional republicanism. Like communists and socialists, progressives wanted an increase in government control, but unlike their big-government cousins, their mode of operation would be through an elitist mindset that would critique the Constitution as an inferior political document that was not up to the challenges of a modern American society. For progressives to achieve their big-government society, they would have to denigrate, ignore, or destroy our Constitution and the Founders who designed it. Progressives call for a transformation of our republican form of government that would in reality be a "regressive" attack on freedom and prosperity. America's Founders not only fought and sacrificed for freedom from regressive big government, they specifically designed a government that if followed faithfully would preserve the liberties we cherish.

The KEY to that republican form of government was it scope and size. It was to be limited; however, not so limited, powerless, and inept like the Articles of Confederation. Our Founders created a limited government strong enough to protect our God-given life and liberties BUT not too BIG to destroy them. Progressives in many cases ignored the original intent of our Founders, arguing that many of the Founders' ideas over time had grown antiquated and ill equipped to handle the social ills of modern man. Going beyond 1776 and 1787, they believed the Constitution needed to "progress" as an evolving or "living constitution" that needed to be molded and if necessary re-written to fit present conditions. R.J. Pestritto, in his excellent book *American Progressivism*, writes:

> Quite simply, the Progressives detested the bedrock principles of American government. They detested the Declaration of Independence, which enshrines the protection of individual natural rights (like property) as the unchangeable purpose of government; and they detested the Constitution, which places permanent limits on the scope of government and is structured in a way that makes the extension of national power beyond its original purpose very difficult. "Progressivism" was, for them, all about progressing, or moving beyond, the principles of our Founders. This is why the Progressives were the first generation of Americans to denounce openly our founding documents. Woodrow Wilson, for example, once warned that "if you want to understand the real Declaration of Independence, do not repeat the preface," i.e. that part of the Declaration which talks about securing individual natural rights as the only legitimate purpose of government. And Theodore Roosevelt, when using the federal government to take over private businesses during the 1902 coal strike, is reported to have remarked, "To hell with the Constitution when people want coal!"

In order to support the "collective" progressive vision, Wilson wants to ignore individual natural rights and Roosevelt wants to circumvent the Constitution!

It is by purposeful design that our Founders established a separation of powers within our three branches of government to create a checks and balances of power that would not allow one branch to grow too powerful in a tyrannical direction. Our Founders, more than anything, wanted us to be a nation under the rule of law; thus the very first article of the Constitution gave much emphasis on the federal government to the legislature or our lawmakers. Then after the legislature came Article 2, or the executive branch, establishing presidential authority and its limitations. Our Founders understood the natural propensity of rulers, executives, and kings to become too BIG for our own good; thus the president was to be second in power and authority with Congress first!

Progressives did not like that idea. Therefore, they set about expanding the power of the executive branch to circumvent congressional laws that they considered regressive and anti-democratic. President Wilson felt that the separation of powers as conceived by our Founders made government slow, impotent, and ineffectual for the tasks of "progressing" American society. Wilson was strongly influenced by Walter Bagehot's 1867 *The English Constitution*, a book that analyzed the nature of the British constitution, the functioning of Parliament and monarchy of the United Kingdom. Forgetting that our Founders fought to be free from the British monarchy and improve upon their system, Wilson saw the United States Constitution as outdated, cumbersome, and corrupt in many ways. He believed, according to one interpreter, that "the U.S. Constitution prevents the government from meeting the country's needs by enumerating rights that the government may not infringe."

In Wilson's book, *Constitutional Government*, he argued that "leadership and control must be lodged somewhere" and, of course, that somewhere was in the presidency where his all-knowing progressive wisdom could connect with the people, assuring democratic justice for all. After all, didn't Thomas Woodrow Wilson have a Ph.D. in history and political science from Johns Hopkins University where his doctoral dissertation, "Congressional Government: A Study in American Politics" concluded that America's Founders were profoundly flawed in their system of congressional governance? Wilson believed that only he and fellow progressives could remedy the constitutional problems with the enlightened insight of a strong executive.

Did we not hear in like manner in 2008 that the Columbia-and Harvard-educated Barack Hussein Obama had a keen "progressive" mind that, combined with other highly educated progressive elites, would change and transform America for the effective advancement and progression of democracy?

Let's be honest. Barack Obama did not create our present BIG government crisis and $15 trillion debt. Both Democrats and Republicans have spent the last fifty years disregarding the Constitution, spending money we don't have, while promising the people that the federal government will solve their problems with other peoples' money. While President Obama did not create the problem, the Democratically controlled Congress, in Obama's first two years, profoundly exacerbated the problems by out-spending the last four presidents combined and by facilitating the explosion of government bureaucratic agencies with more and more supervision in American life. While progressives like Fabians-of-old believe in a gradual evolutionary progress towards their goals, they have, since the election of Barack Obama, accelerated their big-government growth exponentially, and if allowed to remain in office past January 20, 2013, will inevitably transform this great Republic under God into the God of STATISM. Whether it is communism, socialism, or progressivism, they ALL inexorably lead to man's worship of the State as provider and savior. It is no longer as our Founders believed, "In God we Trust," but in "The State we Must!" That is a profoundly anti-republican idea!

Our Founders' Christian worldview held that God owns everything. "The earth is YAHWEH's and all it contains, the world, and those who dwell in it (Psalm 21:1), and YAHWEH-God delegated ownership and dominion of His earth or property to mankind (Genesis 1:26–28). Unlike Karl Marx's belief that the State owns man's property, God's law protects man's ownership of private property and prohibits its theft. The Old and New Testaments confirm this reality. Our Founders abhorred statism! To them the Bible made it perfectly clear: God believes in private property. Karl Marx's *Communist Manifesto* and its socialist adherents believed that private property was an evil idea, and that the State, in replacing God, says: "The earth is the State's, and all it contains, the world, and those who dwell in it."

Our Founders did not have to look too far back in history to learn about a failed experiment in statism or communism. Before leaving England, the Pilgrims unwittingly or naively entered into a land contract with Thomas Weston who instituted a seven-year indentured servitude agreement under the control of a collective or communistic form of enterprise. Weston's company owned all property, and all produce had to go to a common store, from which each individual would receive an equal ration or share regardless of how much he or she had contributed. Any excess produce belonged to the investors, and the Pilgrims' homes and the land they cleared and worked was company property. Under this communistic economic system the Pilgrims received no reward for individual effort and the colony was unable to produce enough food. William Bradford tells us in his book, *On Plymouth Plantation*, that their experiment with a collective or "commune-istic" enterprise was a dismal failure. He writes:

> Experience in this common course among Godly and sober men, may well evidence the vanity that conceit of Plato and other ancients... that the taking away of property, and bringing in community into a common-wealth would make them happy and flourishing, as if they were wiser than God. For this community was found to breed much confusion, discontent and retard much employment... for young men, that were most able and fit for labor and service did complain that they should spend their time and strength to work for other men's wives and children without any recompense... this was thought injustice.

Bradford tells us that he searched the Scriptures for wisdom on what form of enterprise the colony should practice in order to prosper. He writes:

> And for men's wives to be commanded to do service for other men, as dressing their meat, washing their cloths, etc., they deemed it a kind of slavery, neither could many husbands brook it. Upon the point all being to have alike, and all to do alike, they thought themselves in the like condition, and one as good as another; and so, if it did not cut off those relations to God hath set amongst men, yet it did at least diminish and take off the mutual respects that should be preserved amongst them.

William Bradford deduces from hands-on experience, common sense, and the Scriptures that ownership of private property creates incentive and personal responsibility. Bradford argued that socialism was contrary to God's plan for man and that man cannot be expected to labor for no reward. He discovered that their collective experiment made men lazy, irresponsible, and embittered. Humbling themselves before God, Bradford and the Pilgrims saw that practicing utopian communism did not make them wiser than God. Abandoning their socialistic economic experiment and allowing the Pilgrims to own their own parcel of land quickly gave them surplus food, which was sold for other goods and profit.

The Pilgrims' legacy for our Republic under God was not only the Judeo-Christian tradition of Thanksgiving and the necessity of using the Bible for governance, but was also the wisdom in allowing individuals free and private enterprise without the encroachment and control of the State. Our Pilgrim Christian heritage understood that the civil government's function was to protect the marketplace from private coercion or fraud, and that the State's intervention was to be limited and only legitimate where the "enterprise" by free individuals was being violated. Long before Karl Marx and Adam Smith, free enterprise or capitalism had been practiced throughout the colonies creating unprecedented social and economic prosperity.

Unfortunately, this failed socialistic experiment has crept into our churches in the name of social justice, social gospel, progressive Christianity, red-letter Christianity, economic justice, and modern progressivism. These socialistic schemes demand more from the State or the producers and taxpayers, to take the place of personal responsibility and trust in God.

To understand this worship of the State as provider and Savior, we need to understand the growth of progressive socialism in government since the election of progressive socialist President Obama.

CHAPTER 11

PROGRESSIVES AND SOCIALISTS IN GOVERNMENT TODAY

"Socialism is the philosophy of failure, the creed of ignorance and the gospel of envy"
-*Winston Churchill*

"The veil of a happy Democratic governing majority is finally lifted. We didn't have it then; we don't have it now. But what we do have now is a more solidly progressive bunch of Dems in Congress and a president presumably less encumbered by the false illusion that playing nice will get him a date with the other team… throw our support unabashedly behind the Congressional Progressive Caucus, and let's push Obama to finally do the right thing through as many Executive Orders as we can present to him."
-*Karen Dolan, Institute for Policy Studies*

The mid-term elections of 2010 gave hope to liberty as many Americans were awakened by an alarming, aggressive, progressive government expansion and spending by President Obama and his Democratic, socialistic, and progressive allies in Washington, D.C. While many conservative lovers of our Constitution and Founding Fathers were elected, thereby taking control of the House of Representatives, it was not enough to stop the left-wing onslaught of our freedoms. In spite of the 2010 conservative victory, overt and covert tactics and strategies have in many ways continued to expand our federal government. Why?

Aaron Klein's book, *Red Army: The Radical Network That Must Be Defeated To Save America*, observes:

> The 111th Congress, which retired in January 2011, included 316 Democratic Party members. The Democratic Caucus's role is to assist members in achieving consensus and providing the tools necessary to push for and implement their goals. Amid speculation that the House, the eighty-two-member-strong CPC lost only a few members, the CPC actually increased its plurality within the Democratic caucus. In comparison, the conservative Blue Dog Coalition lost half its members. In other words, the election widely seen as repudiating Obama's progressive agenda, the most liberal bloc in Congress, actually gained power.

Gained power!? The left-wing, progressive-socialist BIG government members of Congress gained power in 2010! As the elite media points the finger at conservative Republicans and Democrats as the problem in Washington, D.C., the fact is that the entrenched Radical Left is more entrenched than ever before and has taken over the Democratic Party. How are they doing it?

One way is the CPC. The Congressional Progressive Caucus was co-founded in 1991 by Bernie Sanders, a self-described democratic socialist who had recently been elected to the U.S. House of Representatives and is presently a junior senator from Vermont. The CPC is "organized around the principles of social and economic justice, a nondiscriminatory society, and national priorities which represent the interests of all people, not just the wealthy and powerful." The CPC calls for a more progressive tax system which places a larger portion of the tax burden on corporations and those with higher earnings; a substantial increase in federal funding for social programs designed to meet the needs of low and middle-income American families; "universal access to affordable, high-quality healthcare"; living wage laws; the right of all workers to organize into labor unions and engage in collective bargaining; the legalization of same-sex marriage; U.S. participation in international treaties such as the climate change-related Kyoto Accords; a crackdown on corporate welfare and influence; an increase in income tax rates on upper-middle and upper-class households; tax cuts for the poor; and an increase in welfare spending by the federal government. In other words: BIGGER government and spending money we don't have.

Along with Bernie Sanders and other social democrats, the DSA, or Democratic Socialists of America, were instrumental in creating the CPC. In 1997, top DSA and CPC officials, along with many radical left-wing leaders like AFL-CIO President Richard Trumka, Reverend Jesse Jackson, and socialist professor Noam Chomsky, along with feminist leader Patricia Ireland, met to strategize on how the two groups might be able to "unite our forces on a common agenda." They were able to launch the "Progressive Challenge," a coalition of more than 100 hard-core leftist organizations that sought to unite their activities and objectives under a "multi-issue progressive agenda" that called for bigger government and more spending. By 2002, the Communist Party USA's (CPUSA) political action committee stated that the Progressive Caucus "provides an important lever that can be used to advance workers' issues and move the debate to the Left in every Congressional District in the country." In a 2010 CPUSA report, party member David Bell identified Progressive Caucus members as his organization's "allies in Congress." In 2011, the Congressional Progressive Caucus (CPC) is the largest caucus within the Democratic caucus with eighty-three declared members. The Caucus is co-chaired by representatives Raúl Grijalva (D-AZ) and Keith Ellison (D-MN). Of the twenty standing committees of the House in the 111th Congress, ten were chaired by members of the CPC. Fortunately, those chairmen were replaced when the republicans took control of the House in the 112th Congress. However, with progressive radicals and racists like Raul Grijalva and Keith Ellison in charge of the CPC, much damage can be done to our country. Grijalva has been voted time and time again one of the most big-government, left-wing advocates in Congress and has also been involved with the racist La Raza movement, which calls for a large part of the United States to be returned to Mexico. CPC's other co-chairman, Keith Ellison, has been sworn in on the Koran as the first Muslim elected to Congress who worked for Jew-hating, white-man-hating Louis Farrakhan and his Nation of Islam. Congressman Ellison also supports Muslim Sharia law over American Constitutional law and has close ties to groups like the Muslim American Society, the Council on American-Islamic Relations, and the Islamic Society of North America, all of which are Muslim Brotherhood fronts. It is not a coincidence that the former social democratic speaker of the House and member of the Congressional Progressive Caucus, Nancy Pelosi, worked with San Francisco Democratic Socialists of America in 1995 on the HR 1050 "A Living Wage, Jobs for All Act." On February 11, 1997, Congresswoman Pelosi addressed Congress, paying a tribute to Lenin Peace Prize winner and life-long Communist Party USA member Carlton Goodlett. In 2001, Pelosi took to the pages of the Congressional Record to share her sentiments on the one-hundredth anniversary of Communist Party USA leader Harry Bridges' birth. Here is what she said:

> Harry Bridges was arguably the most significant labor leader of the twentieth century, beloved by the workers of this Nation, and recognized as one of the most important labor leaders in the world... The International Longshoremen's and Warehousemen's Union [was] the most progressive union of the time.

To Ms. Pelosi, this communist-run union was to be admired more than all of the anti-communist unions. It is important to point out that Progressive Congresswoman Nancy Pelosi delivered this glowing speech a full nine years after Bridges' membership in the Communist Party USA Central Committee had been revealed. That same year Pelosi participated in a ribbon-cutting ceremony for the dedication of Harry Bridges Plaza in San Francisco with Mayor Willie Brown.

There are so many affiliations to, and connections with, communists and socialists by many in the Democratic Party that it would take another book to chronicle the collusion of comrades in the progressive cause with cultural Marxists in America. Likewise there are so many alphabet-soup progressive and socialist organizations in alliance with the Democratic Party that it's enough to make your head spin. From the CPC, DSA, CPUSA, PAC, ADA, CLW, NCLR, NOW, NPR, CBPP, CAF, OSI, AV, WPR, AFL-CIO, SEIU, and many, many more, you'd think you were at an Occupy Wall Street rally, Democratic National Convention, or in a Madison, Wisconsin Recall Governor Walker rally.

The Siamese twins of socialism and progressivism have an inextricable symbiotic relationship that advances the cause of statism and cultural Marxism. Unfortunately, many good-hearted Democrats, independents, and Republicans are being fooled into believing that terms like Marxism, socialism, and progressivism are just labels that have little or no relevance to American society. These labels or words are significant in the grand political scheme of things as they are specifically chosen to convey a philosophy of how government and society is to be run in the twenty-first century. As stated in the first chapter, as our Founders designed the United States of America, they very deliberately and specifically chose certain words that would define us as a republican nation under God with limited government to preserve and protect our lives and liberty. The ideas on the size, scope, and form of government behind the words Marxism, socialism, progressivism, and democracy are the antitheses of our Founders' vision. If these labels, derivatives, and cognates have no or little meaning today, then why is it that Democrats and the Columbia and Harvard graduate Barack Hussein Obama use them all the time? That is the topic of our next chapter.

CHAPTER 12

BARACK OBAMA
"THE INTELLECTUAL" FROM
MARX TO ALINSKY

"After the collapse of central planning in Eastern
Europe and the former USSR, the only place in the
world where Marxists were still thriving was the
Harvard political science department."
*-Peter G. Klein, Why Intellectuals Still Support
Socialism*

"If Obama is elected as now seems likely, he'll be the
first real out-of-the-closet intellectual in the White
House in many years."
*-Nicholas Kristof, New York Times, "Obama the
Intellectual"*

John Adams and John Quincy Adams, like Barack Obama,
were educated at Harvard. The profound difference in their
education was while the Adams' learned republican Christian
values, Obama learned from his Marxist professors, Marxist critical theory and brought that anti-American theory to the White
House. Stanley Kurtz writes:

> When I began my research for this book, my inclination
> was to downplay or dismiss evidence of explicit socialism
> in Obama's background. I thought the socialism issue

was an unprovable and unnecessary distraction from the broader question of Obama's ultraliberal inclinations. I was wrong.

"I was wrong," declares Stanley Kurtz in his book, *Radical-in-Chief: Barack Obama and the Untold Story of American Socialism*. After thorough investigation and with copious notes Kurtz concludes:

> From his teenage years under the mentorship of Frank Marshall Davis, to his socialist days at Occidental College, to his life-transforming encounters at New York's Socialist Scholars Conferences, to his immersion in the stealthily socialist community organizing networks of Chicago, Barack Obama has lived in a thoroughly socialist world.

In Obama's 2004 autobiography, *Dreams from My Father*, he very deliberately and specifically says this about his college education:

> I chose my friends carefully. The more politically active black students. The foreign students. The Chicanos. The Marxist professors and structural feminists and punk-rock performance poets. We smoked cigarettes and wore leather jackets. At night in the dorms, we discussed neocolonialism, Franz Fanon, Eurocentrism, and patriarchy... political discussions, the kind at Occidental had once seemed so intense and purposeful, came to take on the flavor of the socialist conferences I sometimes attended at Cooper Union.

Marxist professors, structural feminists, neocolonialism, Franz Fanon, and socialist conferences? Not exactly traditional conservative, republican, Christian topics, individuals, or worldviews. In fact, his educational environment consisted of an array of socialists, anti-colonial militants, radical feminists, progressives, neo-Marxists, Leninists, Maoists, and a who's who list of America's leading big-government advocates. Obama attended the Socialist Scholars Conferences (SSC), which featured the leaders of socialist academia as well as radical revolutionaries, union activists, progressive reformers, and opponents of capitalism. Guest speakers at these conferences included members of the Communist Party USA and the Communist Committees of Correspondence, as well as Maoists, Trotskyists, African-American radicals, radical feminists, and gay activists.

Almost all of Barack Obama's college comrades, tutors, mentors, and colleagues were hard-core, left-wing, big-government ideologues.

Before we cover Barack Obama's big-government worldview, it is important to state that, unlike Karl Marx's very obvious and blatant call for a militant Marxist revolution in the streets, we have explained that Marxism has been molded into various cultural forms and mutations. One key form is its manifestation into what scholars have called cultural Marxism. This form of Marxism, while declawed overtly, is armed covertly with stealth Fabian strategy that utilizes patriotic symbolism, while Marxian and socialistic constructs are covered and clothed in democratic rhetoric. If you listen carefully to Obama and his followers, you can detect the Marxian and socialistic language, actions, and legislation that calls for socialized health care, equal distribution of economic resources, spreading the wealth, paying your fair share, equalizing outcome, and socializing justice.

While an individual may not wear the "horns" of a Marxist devil or fly the communist red flag, he or she can believe in and disseminate Marxian and socialistic values that conflict and contradict our Founders' understanding on how to achieve a free society. I do not believe that Barack Obama, while having hung around with and been taught by Marxists and socialists of various stripes and persuasions throughout his life, is a militant Leninist, Stalinist, or Maoist-Marxist like some of his Chicago community-organizing and college professor friends. But like many of his mentors, Barack Obama without Marxist horns and militancy has been from early on in his life inculcated and indoctrinated with various forms of hard-left, big-government cultural Marxism, socialism, progressivism, and anti-westernism that has shaped his worldview on the function, size, and scope of government in our lives and America's place in the world.

Soon after Obama became president, Evan Thomas, the grandson of six-time Socialist Party presidential candidate Norman Thomas, co-authored a Newsweek cover story titled, "We're All Socialists Now." The article argued that the growth of the federal government coupled with Obama's election was making the U.S. like a European socialist country. Other writers of the Washington Post said that the new president was ushering us into a new age of social democracy while left-wing bloggers like Matthew Yglesias were elated that now we had a real opportunity for "massive socialism."

Writers, historians, political scientists, bloggers, and television commentators all debate what political identification best fits Barack Obama. From terms like democratic socialist, social-democrat, liberal socialist, cultural Marxist, social progressive, neo-Marxist, to neo-socialist and Fabian socialist and many more, Barack Obama has had those terms applied to his worldview due to his big-government advocacy and actions.

Barack Obama is a proud Democrat, who as a Democratic senator voted and helped pass big-government legislation that was farther Left than self-described Socialist Senator Bernie Sanders. As a Democratic president with a Democratic Congress, Barack Obama's first two years in the White House saw spending and government expansion explode at unprecedented levels. As I write this sentence, Obama's government spending and growth continues at an alarming exponential rate.

From early in his life and all the way through his high school, college, and law school years he surrounded himself with Marxist-socialist teachers and mentors. His hero was socialist Saul Alinsky who taught him bottom-up socialistic community organizing. He worked in close association with Marxist-terrorists-turned-education professors, and has had dozens and dozens of socialist, progressive, big-government affiliations, associations, and collegial relationships throughout his life.

Obama is not a believer in our Founding Fathers' vision of a limited republican form of government under God, as his cultural and political worldview preaches economic egalitarianism, punitive progressive taxation, and property redistribution that is to be implemented through large federal government programs that "guarantee" equality of outcome and social justice for all. While the "experts" may debate the various political labels and nuances that apply to Obama, the bottom line is that Barack Obama's form of government under himself is unlimited with faith in an intellectual elite and ultimate trust in the State to solve America's problems. That is categorically and undeniably an anti-republican form of government under God.

When President Reagan, in the spirit of Thomas Jefferson's "the government that governs best governs least" philosophy, stated in his 1981 inaugural address that "government is not the solution to our problem; government is the problem," he, like our Founders, realized that one of the biggest sources of mankind's problems is government.

Big Government.

This understanding of our Founders' view of government is crucial for America today. As explained earlier, our Founders were not stupid anarchists who advocated no government, nor were they arrogant statists who believed they could solve all of America's problems through their collective wisdom as implemented by the long arm of the State. Citizen Ronald Reagan articulated this reality in his classic 1964 Barry Goldwater presidential election speech, "Time for Choosing," when he said:

> This is the issue of this election: whether we believe in our capacity for self-government or whether we abandon the American Revolution and confess that a little intellectual elite in a far-distant capitol can plan our lives for us better than we can plan them ourselves.

Senator Obama, during the 2008 election, was hailed as an intellectual giant from Columbia and Harvard who was going to meet the needs of the masses by spreading the wealth and creating social justice throughout the land through the power of centralized government planning from Washington, D.C. Again, Ronald Reagan understood that worldviews like Obama's were:

> The very thing the Founding Fathers sought to minimize. They knew that governments don't control things. A government can't control the economy without controlling people. And they know when a government sets out to do that, it must use force and coercion to achieve its purpose. They also knew, those Founding Fathers, that outside of its legitimate functions, government does nothing as well or as economically as the private sector of the economy.

That is why Barack Obama easily fits into the category of a big-government socialist. His educational, community, and political track record is a megaphone that speaks loud and clear as to his controlling intentions for Americans. While many may conclude that his intentions are good, they are the path to our republic's end.

There are many well-researched and documented books that cover President Obama's dangerous, radical worldview and connections. What follows is just a brief overview.

I will cover what some might call incidentals or minor associations, but I would argue that these incidentals reflect an affinity and attraction to like-minded worldviews and philosophies. By endorsements, social interaction, common symbolism, nomenclature, organizations, or enemies, these associations connect Barack Obama to a wide variety of activities, events, and people that do not fit into the category of traditional Judeo-Christian republican values and instead align themselves on the Left, Hard Left, and Radical Left of the political spectrum. While some associations are casual and others are intimate and prolonged relationships, their common denominator is why they are tied together in some form or fashion.

His father, Barack Hussein Obama Sr., was an African socialist whose writings included a research project called "Problems With Our Socialism," which advocated 100 percent taxation of the rich, communal ownership of land, and the forced confiscation of privately controlled land. His mother, Stanley Ann Dunham, was a '60s radical feminist and atheist who was on the hard-left side of the political spectrum. Barack said of his mother, "the values she taught me continue to be my touchstone when it comes to how I go about the world of politics."

In *Dreams From My Father*, Obama affectionately refers to "Frank" as a mentor in his teen years in Hawaii from 1971 to 1979.

Barack developed a close relationship with Frank, listening to his poetry and getting advice on his career path. Frank was Frank Marshall Davis, a very popular member of the Communist Party USA. University of Hawaii Professor Kathryn Takara's dissertation on the life of Frank Marshall Davis confirms Frank Davis as having a significant influence on Obama when he attended Punahou Prep High School in Hawaii from 1975 to 1979.

Called by Obama "Uncle J," the Reverend Jeremiah Wright was Barack's pastor and mentor for twenty years at Trinity United Church of Christ in Chicago, and he had also married Barack and Michelle and baptized their two children. The philosophy of Wright's church is based on the teachings of James Cone's 1969 Black Liberation Theology, which is a mix of black culture, Christianity, and Marxist philosophy. Cone has stated that Rev. Wright's church represents an accurate interpretation of his liberation theology. Among the ideas expressed by Cone is the notion that "black religion and Marxist philosophy may show us the way to build a completely new society." Cone taught that "to be black is to be committed to destroying everything this country loves and adores," and that is the Judeo-Christian worldview and America's republican form of government. The highly educated Columbia and Harvard graduate Barack Obama attended Rev. Wright's church for twenty years, absorbing his Marxist worldview and never complained about the vicious, anti-white, anti-Jewish, anti-capitalist, and anti-American diatribes that filled the pulpit. Wright's anti-American sermons created a media controversy that eventually exposed one of Obama's mentors as a radical left-wing Marxist racist. At first Obama defended his "Uncle," until his poll numbers fell precipitously, and in classic Machiavellian style, Senator Obama threw his "Uncle" under the bus and denounced him in the spring of 2008, after twenty years of friendship. Rev. Wright has also worked with the Jew-hating, white-man-hating Nation of Islam leader, Louis Farrakhan. Wright's church's magazine, Trumpet, has given Farrakhan a lifetime achievement award and Farrakhan has appeared on it's cover with then Senator Barack Obama.

While Chicago may have the Bears, this Green Bay Packers fan thinks Chicago is a great town with a sweet Midwest feel of hospitality and kindness. With that being said, it is the town of Al Capone, Frank Nitti, the Mafia, and some of the most corrupt politics in the history of America. In his book, *Red Chicago*, Randi Storch describes how Marxism had influenced and taken over much of Chicago's political world in the 1930s. It is still like that today as a variety of social and political organizations throughout Chicago espouse some form of socialist, Marxist, progressive, big-government programs. It is not by accident that Obama chose Chicago to be "his kind of town." Obama was handpicked by Chicago Marxist politician Alice Palmer to succeed her in the Illinois state senate. Nine years before Palmer picked Obama to be her successor, she was the only African-American journalist to travel to the Soviet Union to attend the 27th Congress of the USSR, and according to an article Palmer wrote in the CPUSA newspaper, she gave a glowing report on Soviet society as compared to oppressive American society.

Obama's run for the Illinois state senate was launched at a fundraiser organized at the Chicago home of Bill Ayers and Bernardine Dohrn. Ayers and Dohrn, as we discussed in chapter eight, were Marxist revolutionary terrorists from the Weather Underground, and after coming out of hiding became cultural Marxists in the college classroom. Bill Ayers served for six years on the Chicago Annenberg Challenge (CAC) with Barack Obama. Both men headed up separate branches of the CAC that worked together on project funding. They also served together on the board of the Woods Fund. During this time period Professor Ayers wrote a book on the juvenile justice system, which was endorsed wholeheartedly by Obama. When originally asked about his endorsement of Ayers' book Obama denied it. Barack Obama also taught classes at the University of Illinois-Chicago, where Ayers was a faculty member until 2010. In 2002, the Black Radical Congress hosted a panel discussion at the University of Illinois-Chicago called "Intellectuals in Times of Crisis." Marxist Bill Ayers, three endorsers of the Black Radical Congress, and Illinois State Senator Barack Obama were on this panel. As mentioned in chapter eight, Bill Ayers' wife Bernardine Dohrn was the leader of the Revolutionary Youth Movement of the SDS and the Weather Underground. Bernardine worked at Sidley & Austin, after coming out of the underground, the law firm where

Michelle Obama worked. Dohrn is currently employed as an adjunct professor at Northwestern University.

Stanley Kurtz, in his article "Inside Obama's Acorn," states that Obama had a long-term relationship with the anti-capitalist group ACORN:

> Obama has had an intimate and long-term association with the Association of Community Organizations for Reform Now (Acorn)... Chicago Acorn appears to have played a major role in Obama's political advance... Acorn's radical agenda sometimes shifts toward "undisguised authoritarian socialism."

Committees of Correspondence (CoC or CofC) began in late 1991, when about one-third of the Communist Party USA membership split from the party and joined with former Maoists, Trotskyites, socialists, and anarchists to form a new organization. Their official founding conference was held in Chicago in 1994. In 2000, Committees of Correspondence became Committees of Correspondence for Democracy and Socialism (CCDS). The CoC worked with Obama in Chicago through the Marxist New Party and Alice Palmer's campaign. In 2008, CoC actively campaigned for Obama and several supporters were endorsers of the "Progressives for Obama" website. Manning Marable, CCDS leader, writing in the December 2008 issue of British Trotskyite journal Socialist Review, explained Obama's relationship to the Marxist Chicago Left:

What makes Obama different is that he has also been a community organizer. He has read left literature, including my works, and he understands what socialism is. A lot of the people working with him are, indeed, socialists with backgrounds in the Communist Party or as independent Marxists. There are a lot of people like that in Chicago who have worked with him for years.

Marable was referring to the numerous former Chicago Communist Party USA members working with Obama who had become members or supporters of Committees of Correspondence.

Obama went to several political meetings with the Democratic Socialists in Chicago and was endorsed by them. Cliff Kincaid, in his article "Is Barack Obama a Marxist Mole?" writes:

Obama's socialist backing goes back at least to 1996, when he received the endorsement of the Chicago branch of the Democratic Socialists of America (DSA) for an Illinois state senate seat. Later, the Chicago DSA newsletter reported that Obama, as a state senator, showed up to eulogize Saul Mendelson, one of the "champions" of Chicago's democratic left and a long-time socialist activist. Obama's stint as a "community organizer" in Chicago has gotten some attention, but his relationship with the DSA socialists, who groomed and backed him, has been generally ignored.

Many Obama supporters and campaign workers idolized Communist Che Guevara and while campaigning for Obama wore Che T-shirts or used his flag in their Obama headquarters. Che, known as "the Butcher of La Cabana Prison" for murdering thousands of innocent Cubans, helped advance Cuban Marxism and worked with Castro in bringing to Cuba the Soviet nuclear ballistic missiles that caused the Cuban Missile Crisis in October 1962. Che told the British newspaper Daily Worker some weeks later, "if the missiles had been under Cuban control, they would have fired them against major U.S. cities."

Obama proudly endorsed Socialist Senator Bernie Sanders and has hired a number of self-described communists and admirers of Marxist mass murderer Mao Zedong, such as his Green Czar Van Jones and White House Communication Director Anita Dunn. While endorsements by the Communist Party USA and other socialist organizations does not make Obama a hard-core socialist, it does reflect his big-government kinship with them.

The key mentor in shaping Obama's Machiavellian worldview is not the Jewish atheist Karl Marx, but the Jewish atheist and cultural Marxist Saul Alinsky.

Bert Kjos, in his analysis of *Rules for Radicals* by Saul Alinsky 1971, writes:

> Alinsky's tactics were based, not on Stalin's revolutionary violence, but on the Neo-Marxist strategies of Antonio Gramsci, an Italian Communist. Relying on gradualism, infiltration, and the dialectic process rather than a bloody revolution, Gramsci's transformational Marxism was so subtle that few even noticed the deliberate changes. Alinsky followed Gramsci, not Lenin. In fact, Gramsci aroused Stalin's wrath by suggesting that Lenin's revolutionary plan wouldn't work in the West. Instead the primary assault would be on Biblical absolutes and

Christian values, which must be crushed as a social force before the new face of Communism could rise and flourish. Malachi Martin gave us a progress report: By 1985, the influence of traditional Christian philosophy in the West was weak and negligible... Gramsci's master strategy was now feasible. Humanly speaking, it was no longer too tall an order to strip large majorities of men and women in the West of those last vestiges that remained to them of Christianity's transcendent God.

Alinsky, like Gramsci, hated Christianity and America's devotion to biblical Christianity as the inspiration and foundation of our republican form of government. Saul Alinsky's "master strategy" was to mold Marxism into a practical, plausible idea that would, through grassroots community organizations, infiltrate society and spread socialism. Born in "Red Chicago," Alinsky studied criminology as a graduate student at the University of Chicago, during which time he became friendly with the Mafia kingpins Al Capone and Frank Nitti. After Capone went to prison, Alinsky tells us that Nitti "took me under his wing. I called him Professor and I became his student." Alinsky's studies under Nitti and some of his socialist professors at the University of Chicago taught him that criminal problems were not a character problem but were caused by an unjust capitalistic system where the "haves" drove the "have-nots" to crime.

Stanley Kurtz writes in his 2010 book *Radical in Chief*:

Alinsky was... convinced that large-scale socialist transformation would require an alliance between the struggling middle class and the poor. The key to radical social change, Alinsky thought, was to turn the wrath of America's middle class against large corporations.

Sounds like the Occupy movement to me, but more on that later.

Alinsky's "large scale socialist transformation" would come through the deliberate and well-thought-out application of his 1971 book *Rules for Radicals*. Alinsky dedicates his book to Lucifer, "the first radical," thus revealing to us the "mind" of a wise stealth serpent. Alinsky says this about Satan in his dedication:

> Lest we forget, an over-the-shoulder acknowledgement to the very first radical: from all our legends, mythology, and history... the first radical known to man who rebelled against the establishment and did so effectively that at least won his own kingdom—Lucifer.

Rebellion against the establishment, the Judeo-Christian Republic-under-God establishment, was the rule of the day. According to Alinsky this radical rebellion needed to tone down covert Marxian rhetoric and overt revolutionary activity. New Left radicals like Bill Ayers, John Jacobs, Tom Hayden, and Abbie Hoffman used stupid "revolutionary rhetoric" like "Up against the wall motherf-ker," "destroy Amerika," and "kill the pigs" to announce to the whole world their militant-Marxist intentions. Alinsky writes: "the failure of many of our younger activists to understand the art of communications has been disastrous" and was almost always futile. Alinsky taught his disciples that deception and lying was the key. Alinsky's "rules" were to be used by his followers in Trojan horse-Fabian stealth style, as author Richard Poe puts it in his article "The Chicago Connection: Hillary, Obama and the Cult of Alinsky":

> Alinsky viewed revolution as a slow, patient process. The trick was to penetrate existing institutions such as churches, unions, and political parties. He advised organizers and their disciples to quietly, subtly gain influence within the decision-making ranks of these institutions, and to introduce changes from that platform. ...Alinsky scolded the Sixties Left for scaring off potential converts in Middle America. True revolutionaries do not flaunt their radicalism, Alinsky taught. They cut their hair, put on suits, and infiltrate the system from within.

The Alinsky model was to sell socialism as "progressivism," "social justice," "social democracy," and "economic democracy."

It is important to understand why Barack Obama's and Hillary Clinton's socialist mentor Saul Alinsky dedicated his book to Satan. The Scriptures tell us that Satan, or Lucifer, is a deceiver and will use many devious and deceitful tactics to fool his enemies—God and mankind. Marx loved the words of Mephistopheles in Faust: "Everything in existence is worth being destroyed." To be "radical" for Alinsky, in the style and spirit of Satan, was "to destroy the values, structures, and institutions that sustain the society in which we live." For America, that would be our republican form of government under the God of Abraham, Isaac, and Jacob, the God of Israel, the God of the Bible.

The multifaceted and deceitful nature of Satan, with his multiple names and disguises, reflects the way the Radical Left camouflages their agenda by using a wide variety of names like socialists, social democrats, liberals, new leftists, democrats, social justice activists, and progressives. In the past, many members of the Communist Party USA did not call themselves communists but progressives. In 1948, under the influence of the Soviet Union and the CPUSA, the Progressive Party was created with FDR's ex-vice president Henry Wallace as their candidate to go up against Harry S. Truman. In the 1940s with Henry Wallace and in 1972 with the Democratic campaign of George McGovern, the progressives penetrated and influenced the Democratic Party and, as discussed earlier, they are doing so today with President Obama in a much greater efficacious capacity. Satan was the first progressive-Marxist prototype as he tempted Adam and Eve to destroy the established order, the Garden of Eden, by rebellion against God and His laws so they could "be as gods." Satan and the socialistic vision is to create a "New World," a "New Man," free from any oppressive social structure and form of government that trusts in God for guidance and limits the capacity of government to achieve an earthly 'utopia.'

Alinsky is known as the father of community organizing. His book, *Rules for Radicals*, outlines many of the radical tactics used today in community organizing campaigns that rely on street-agitation tactics such as the Industrial Areas Foundation, which trained Obama in organizing tactics. Obama worked with the

Developing Communities Project and the Socialist Gamaliel Foundation, both inspired by Saul Alinsky's tactics and cultural-Marxist philosophy. Barack Obama even wrote a chapter on community organizing in the book *After Alinsky*. Saul Alinsky's son, Lee David Alinsky, in 2008 praised Obama on his ability to carry out his father's radical rules, saying that Barack "learned his lesson well."

Now to the question of guilt by association.

We have heard over and over again that "guilt by association," otherwise known as "association fallacy," is "an inductive, informal fallacy of the type of hasty generalization or red herring which asserts that qualities of one thing are inherently qualities of another, merely by an irrelevant association." While I would concur that far too often political pundits on both the Left and Right are guilty of "hasty guilt-by-association fallacies," we must strive through discernment, intellectual honesty, scrutinizing evaluation, and verification to determine whether the association is relevant and indicting, or irrelevant and just a simple, harmless, social connection or coincidence. Just because a number of Barack Obama followers wear the Marxist murderer Che Guevara T-shirt and put his poster in Obama campaign headquarters does not mean Obama is a militant Marxist who condones Castro's communism. It might mean his followers are "useful idiots" or that they believe Obama's Marxism matches theirs, but it is not enough evidence to indict.

However, if you have a preponderance of evidence that points to a preponderant number of relationships, friendships, companionships, and mentorships, along with politicians, professors, and educational and community associations that share a common worldview, vision, values, and ultimate goal of a "just society," there is a great and profound probability you are guilty as charged.

As a covert Fabian Marxist you will probably cry out, "That is an association fallacy! I am not a socialist! I am not a Marxist!" However, if you are an overt Marxist you would declare, "I am guilty as charged! And proud to say so! I am a socialist! I am a Marxist! I associate with these people and organizations because we are of like mind with the same worldview, vision, values, and ultimate goal of a 'just society.'" It is important to note that the dictionary definition of association is:

1. a group of people having a common purpose or interest; a society or club

2. the act of associating or the state of being associated

3. friendship or companionship

4. a mental connection of ideas, feelings, or sensations: association of revolution with bloodshed

When you study and analyze Barack Hussein Obama's friendships, companions, political connections, and the groups of people he has hung out with and worked with throughout his life, they have a "common purpose and mental connection of ideas."

That main idea, that common purpose, is socialism, cultural Marxism, or central-planning control by big government.

From Marxist mentors like Frank Marshall Davis, his college professors, his "Uncle" Pastor Rev. Wright, and his socialist idol Saul Alinsky, to militant Marxists like Bill Ayers and Bernardine Dohrn, Obama's worldview on government structure, functioning, and design is undoubtedly in the socialist-cultural-Marxist camp. It may be covert, clandestine, and Fabian, but it is socialist and Marxist nonetheless. Writer Jack Dee of Colorful Times summarizes Obama's communist connections brilliantly when he states:

> All of these incestuous relationships directly place Barack Obama deep inside the socialist/communist movements in Chicago. His plans and policies are radical and his associations and partners are mostly on the very far left of politics. Socialism and communism are not—and shouldn't be—acceptable philosophies in this country, especially from a person running for president. This isn't simply a matter of "guilt by association." These relationships are long-lasting and ingrained into Barack's political philosophy and ideology. There's a reason why he will do anything and everything it takes to ignore, deny, or denounce every one of these associations once they are brought to the public's attention. Is this guilt by association? Not at all. These associations demonstrate a pattern of relationships with leftist radicals, criminally corrupt developers, and racially divisive activists. These relationships are not a matter of happenstance either. Barack sought out these groups from his early days. He did not grow up in Chicago—he chose to live there. His associations are a direct result of his decision-making and his chosen path to political power. He willingly

participated in socialist-minded groups and worked with radicals and unrepentant criminals. He is beyond dangerous to this republic of ours and his policies are beyond destructive.

Yes, Jack, President Obama is beyond dangerous to this republic and that is why concerned Americans who love this Republic under God MUST take action to educate and inform other Americans on the great danger that lurks in the land. This cultural and political war needs now more than ever a citizen army equipped with knowledge—politically incorrect knowledge but historically correct knowledge—on our Founders, on constitutional republicanism, and on how the Judeo-Christian worldview and Scriptures guided and shaped the founding of the Unites States.

There is hope in this war.

Millions of Americans have joined Tea Partiers, Conservatives, Constitutionalists, Traditionalists, Libertarians, and a number of Christian churches who are not afraid to lose their 501(c)(3) status and are willing to count the cost to "proclaim liberty throughout the land."

While we may be winning a few battles here and there in this war, we are losing far too many cultural and political battles as a myriad of wolf packs in sheep's clothing scour the land looking for unsuspecting sheep to consume. These wolves live in the White House, in Congress, and in our government schools and unions, and they are growing daily.

While we know that knowledge is power, we also know that the education establishment in America is a cultural-Marxist ally of Barack Obama. One of the biggest supporters of Obama's anti-republican vision is America's biggest union, the National Education Association (NEA). The NEA loves Obama's big-government, trillion-dollar spending programs that help them continue their campaign to indoctrinate America's youth with an anti-Christian worldview.

In 2010, the NEA website shocked many when they recommended for America's public schoolteachers two books by Obama's mentor, Saul Alinsky, *Reveille for Radicals* and *Rules for Radicals*. When Americans across the country protested such audacious endorsements of a radical left-winger, the NEA very quietly took the recommendations off their website.

Let us turn to the NEA and their nefarious mode of operation in our culture and schools.

CHAPTER 13

NATIONAL EDUCATION ASSOCIATION: UNION POWER OVER THE CHILDREN

"The schools cannot allow parents to influence the kind of values-education their children receive in school; that is what is wrong with those who say there is a universal system of values. Our (humanistic) goals are incompatible with theirs."
-Paul Haubner, Specialist for the NEA

"The battle for mankind's future must be waged and won in the public school classroom. The classroom must and will become an arena of conflict between the old and the new—the rotting corpse of Christianity and the new faith of humanism."
-The Humanist magazine, January-February 1983, John Dunphy

Not only is the National Education Association one the biggest contributors and supporters of Barack Obama, who is one of the most hard-core, left-wing socialist presidents in America's history, but the NEA's humanist, anti-Christian agenda is one of the biggest contributors to the destruction of our Republic under God since the Japanese bombed Pearl Harbor seventy years ago. The war that concerns me now more than the overt bombs of the enemy are the covert cultural bombs of the NEA within our schools that are exploding in the minds of America's children in the classroom. A classic example of the NEA's attempt to finish off the "rotting corpse of Christianity and advance the faith of humanism" is seen in NEA representative Diane Schneider, a Ramapo High School health teacher and a leader of the Gay Lesbian and Straight Education Network (GLSEN).

Ms. Schneider does training workshops for the NEA and trains trainers in Lesbian, Gay, Bisexual, and Transgender (LGBT) awareness and sensitivity. Representing the NEA, Schneider was asked by the United Nations Population Fund (UNFPA) to speak and train on combating homophobia and transphobia in American schools. Schneider called for more "inclusive" sex education in U.S. public schools while advocating cross-dressing and the teaching of oral sex, masturbation, and orgasms in the classroom. She claimed that the idea of sex education remains an oxymoron if it is abstinence-based or if students are still able to opt out. Schneider stressed that comprehensive sex education is "the only way to combat heterosexism and gender conformity... and we must make these issues a part of every middle and high-school student's agenda." This rejection of the universal Judeo-Christian value system and the undermining of the traditional values of millions of American parents is commonplace at NEA teaching and training conferences all across America and is perpetuated by its affiliates and public schools from New York to California.

This cultural and political warfare was exemplified on July 6, 2009, at the NEA's national convention in San Diego, California.

Robert Chanin, after forty-one years as the National Education Association's chief lawyer, gave a shocking and revealing farewell speech that tore the sheep's clothing off the NEA's wolf-pack socialistic agenda. Here are a few excerpts from his caustic but revealing speech and my comments interspersed:

> Why are these conservative and right-wing bastards picking on NEA and its affiliates? I will tell you why: It is the price we pay for success. NEA and its affiliates have been singled out because they are the most effective unions in the United States. And they are the nation's leading advocates for public education and the type of liberal social and economic agenda that these groups find unacceptable...

This "right-wing conservative bastard" has fought the NEA and Wisconsin Education Association Council from the first day I taught in a Wisconsin public school in the 1980s. From day one I knew they were powerful and effective at advancing their left-wing, politically correct, cultural-Marxist, liberal social and economic agenda. You could see, feel, and hear the NEA-WEAC omnipresence in the classroom, at teaching conventions, and at faculty meetings.

Chanin again:

> At first glance, some of you may find these attacks troubling. But you would be wrong. They are, in fact, really a good thing. When I first came to NEA in the early '60s it had few enemies and was almost never criticized, attacked, or even mentioned in the media. This was

because no one really gave a damn about what NEA did, or what NEA said. It was the proverbial sleeping giant: a conservative, a political, do-nothing organization. But then, NEA began to change. It embraced collective bargaining. It supported teacher strikes. It established a political action committee. It spoke out for affirmative action. It defended gay and lesbian rights. What NEA said and did began to matter. And the more we said and did, the more we pissed people off. And, in turn, the more enemies we made. So the bad news, or depending on your point of view, the good news, is that NEA and its affiliates will continue to be attacked by conservative and right-wing groups as long as we continue to be effective advocates for public education, for education employees, and for human and civil rights.

Did you notice how the NEA's top lawyer discussed how the NEA wasn't criticized and had few enemies when he came on board in the early '60s?

This not just a coincidence.

It was in the '60s that there was a manifestation of a "counter-cultural coming of age." The covert underground world of socialism and its variant lifestyles and political worldviews were now bold enough to overtly demand power and money. Instead of focusing on education, this national association began to associate with the main counter-culture power players to expand its own power, influence, and pocketbook. They embraced the socialistic mode of power through collective bargaining. They embraced illegal teacher strikes at the expense of the children. They embraced gay and lesbian so-called rights, and they became one the most power-ful political-action players in America as they had the Democratic Party in the palm of their hand.

Chanin again:

> And that brings me to my final and most important point, which is why, at least in my opinion, NEA and its affiliates are such effective advocates. Despite what some among us would like to believe, it is not because of our creative ideas. It is not because of the merit of our positions. It is not because we care about children. And it is not because we have a vision of a great public school for every child. NEA and its affiliates are effective advocates because we have power. And we have power because there are more than 3.2 million people who are willing to pay us hundreds of millions of dollars in dues each year because they believe that we are the unions that can most effectively represent them, the unions that can protect their rights and advance their interests as education employees.

> This is not to say that the concern of NEA and its affili-ates with closing achievement gaps, reducing dropout rates, improving teacher quality, and the like are un-important or inappropriate. To the contrary, these are the goals that guide the work we do. But they need not and must not be achieved at the expense of due process, employee rights, and collective bargaining. That simply is too high a price to pay! When all is said and done, NEA and its affiliates must never lose sight of the fact that they are unions, and what unions do first and foremost is represent their members.

"It is not because we care about children… it is because we have power." These words by the top lawyer for the NEA are the embodiment of cultural Marxism's worldview and philosophy. Power! The power to intimidate, the power to indoctrinate, the power to initiate social engineering, and essentially the power to confiscate citizens' money to fill the coffers of NEA bureaucrats and teachers' pocketbooks across America. This NEA left-wing power agenda is why American government schools are having profound achievement gaps, dropout rates, and a number of bad teachers in the classroom dumbing down our children. Chanin rationalizes that it is more important to be concerned about due process, employee rights, and collective bargaining than the education of our youth.

There is an important point I don't want you to miss about Chanin's flippant and arrogant NEA attitude. He states that 3.2 million teachers are willing to pay their dues each year.

"Willing!?" Poppycock to that balderdash and twaddle!

I fought from day one to not have my money taken by the corrupt NEA-WEAC. I was never willing to give my money or have the citizens who paid my wages give money to an organization that has an agenda more in line with the likes of Saul Alinsky, Jimmy Carter, Karl Marx, and John Dewey than our Founding Fathers! As a Wall Street Journal editorial noted, the NEA's financial disclosure forms "expose the union as a honeypot for left-wing political causes that have nothing to do with teachers, much less students."

Here is a list of the left-wing organizations that are recipients of teachers' forced NEA dues:

- ACORN

- American Rights at Work

- Americans United for Separation of Church and State

- Asian American Legal Defense and Education Fund

- Asian Pacific American Labor Alliance

- Ballot Initiative Strategy Center

- Business and Professional Women/USA

- Campaign for America's Future

- Center for Community Change

- Center for Policy Alternatives

- Children's Defense Fund

- Communities for Quality Education

- Communities United to Strengthen America

- Congressional Black Caucus Foundation

- Congressional Hispanic Caucus Institute

- Democratic GAIN

- Democratic Leadership Council

- Early Vote Denver

- Economic Policy Institute

- Gay, Lesbian and Straight Education Network

- GLAAD

- Human Rights Campaign

- Joint Center for Political and Economic Studies

- Labor Council for Latin American Advancement

- Latina Initiative

- Leadership Conference on Civil Rights

- League of Rural Voters

- Mexican American Legal Defense and Educational Fund

- NAACP

- National Association for Bilingual Education

- National Council of La Raza

- National Partnership for Women & Families

- National Women's Law Center

- People for the American Way

- Rainbow PUSH Coalition

- Sierra Club

- Southern Christian Leadership Conference

- The Citizenship Project

- The National Coalition on Black Civic Participation

- The Task Force Foundation

- USAction

- Women's Campaign Forum

- Women's Voices, Women Vote

- Working America

And, of course, Barack Obama's 2008 and 2012 presidential campaigns.

Studies have shown that a large percentage of NEA's membership is conservative, Republican, and Christian, and if they could they would not pay union dues to an organization whose values they disagree with. But against their wishes their money is taken out of their paychecks automatically once they start teaching. The facts show that when "paycheck protection" laws require unions to get permission from teachers before taking money for political purposes, teachers almost always say "no." According to Teachers' Unions Exposed:

> When teachers were given the chance to opt out of paying for the political causes of education unions, the number of teachers participating in Utah dropped from 68 percent to 6.8 percent, and the number of represented teachers contributing in Washington dropped from 82 percent to 6 percent. Predictably, union officials fight tooth and nail against "paycheck protection" laws that

give teachers a real choice about how their money is spent.

When Indiana Governor Mitch Daniels ended collective bargaining and the automatic collection of dues in 2005, the number of members paying dues plummeted by roughly 90 percent. I know from my own experience in Wisconsin, that when Governor Walker ended most collective bargaining and automatic collection of dues, a number of teachers opted out but were very quiet about exercising that right over concerns of negative reaction by colleagues. Even NEA top lawyer Robert Chanin understood that reality when he spoke in a U.S. district court oral argument in 1978:

> It is well-recognized that if you take away the mechanism of payroll deduction, you won't collect a penny from these people, and it has nothing to do with voluntary or involuntary. I think it has to do with the nature of the beast, and the beasts who are our teachers... simply don't come up with the money regardless of the purpose.

"The beasts who are the teachers?!" Once again this bumptious NEA lawyer denigrates and belittles teachers who are not willing to fill the pockets of NEA bureaucrats, many of whom make well over six figures and use our money for left-wing progressive and socialistic causes. This is no different than FDR's progressive move during World War II to collect federal income tax through payroll deduction, but then this was never removed. The NEA knows that the lifeline of their lucrative left-wing cash cow is the payroll deduction method, which automatically takes taxpayers' dollars regardless of what the taxpayers think about that. That is, as Thomas Jefferson said, tyranny pure and simple, and I salute governors like Walker and Daniels who are willing to fight such corruption!

Patty Degen, a forty-two-year career public school teacher, in her brave book, *The Greatest Story of Fraud and Deception Never Read*, speaks candidly about the intimidation and thuggery of the NEA:

> The NEA started out innocently in 1857 in Philadelphia and the AFT in 1916 in Illinois, but both have been transformed into brass-knuckled labor unions. "Sometimes when you're standing on the line and you got a brick in your hand, you have to throw it. Then it's up to the union lawyers to get you out!" –William Winpisinger, former union president. I mentioned the million-dollar image campaigns they conduct, but there's something else. Particularly, the NEA cleverly and deceptively changes its stripes depending on the community—none of the thug tactics are used in upscale communities where the high property taxes make their activities a piece of cake. Not so in lower tax areas. I personally saw what the unions did in New Brighton, PA, when a store owner on the school board had a brick or two thrown through his store's plate-glass window when he would not vote for teacher raises. Teachers often forget that when they get pay raises, their property taxes go up, too. Perhaps, all in all, being a union member isn't worth all that much! On top of that, a high percentage of public school teachers send their own children to private schools, as many as 25% or more. There are instances when union

"thugs" key people's cars or order a load of manure to be dumped on an opponent's front yard. These cases never seem to be prosecuted. I personally suffered from this union mentality that some people nurture: a relative withheld distributions to me from my brother's estate mainly because she knew I was opposed to teachers' unions, and she had taken part in a strike in the above-mentioned town.

The union fights attempts to limit taxes, cut government spending, and even to curb illegal immigration. It's no wonder then that union bureaucrats at the Department of Education (Just think, the NEA has its own cabinet office!) write all these bilingual programs. All these relationships give the NEA access to public policy-making, which is arguably unconstitutional. Labor allies like FDR long opposed public-sector unionization because of the potential for abuse (Boy, was he ever right!), but these scruples were abandoned around 1960 when federal employee collective bargaining was first allowed. The NEA's structure is DECEPTIVE, thus hiding the truth from the American public. It is highly centralized, but its public face is local.

How is it that the NEA gained so much power and money? I still remember reading the November-December 1980 NEA magazine Today's Education, with President Jimmy Carter on the cover, and wondering how a theoretically pluralistic, fair, and balanced education association could endorse any candidate so blatantly. As I researched the NEA, what I discovered blew me away as to their values, political connections, communist affiliations, activities, and very anti-America worldview. I attended Arizona State University in the 1970s, and with Arizona being a right-to-work state I never experienced coercion or intimidation at my non-education jobs. After getting my degree in biblical studies at Arizona College of the Bible, I moved back to my home state of Wisconsin, and while substitute teaching throughout the Fox Valley area, I slowly began to see and feel the power of the NEA-WEAC. After completing a graduate degree in Judeo-Christian Studies at Ashland Theological Seminary in Ohio, I landed an American History teaching job at a Wisconsin public high school in 1988, the last year of Ronald Reagan's presidency. I knew something was awry when on the first day I put a picture of President Reagan in my classroom and a number of teachers made negative comments with some telling me to take it down or tear it up. When I noticed the NEA-WEAC dues taken out of my first few paychecks, I began to intensify my NEA-WEAC research on how they could get away with the confiscation of my and the taxpayers' money. Unlike many teachers, I read word for word NEA literature and studied their bylaws, their purpose statements, their values, worldview, and agenda. The more knowledge I gained the more disturbed I was at the radicalness of their agenda and purpose. The last thing the NEA-WEAC wants is for educators to be educated on the NEA. How ironic, duplicitous, and hypocritical.

A so-called "educational" association against educators being educated on the issues.

There is a fundamental reason for that. The NEA thrives and survives on naivety, ignorance, intimidation, and what I call "teacher think." Monopolies, totalitarians, and tyrannies so reflective of socialism and Marxism do not want free and independent thinkers. They need, they orchestrate, they demand "collective" group-think or "teacher think." Being the "beasts" that we are, we have to be passive sheep that are molded into the image of the union. We are expected to be automatons that regurgitate the party line. If we dare cross that line we are scolded and reminded of our proper place in that line. This Democratic Party line is perpetuated and reinforced in Pavlovian form by our education departments at American universities and colleges, where left-wing social democrats and socialist and Marxist professors indoctrinate future teachers on what to think, what not to think and say, and especially what to teach. If I had a dollar for every student teacher or raw, right-out-of-college teacher who fell in line either through naivety, ignorance, intimidation, or his or her own party-line, left-wing indoctrination, I'd be rich! In my experiences in the political science, history, and social studies departments at Arizona State, the University of Wisconsin-Oshkosh, and Madison, almost all the faculty were hard-core, left-wing advocates and supporters of the NEA, ACLU, big government, secular progressivism, socialism, and the Democratic Party. Most of my professors and the overwhelming majority of professors in American universities are not shy about their left-wing political worldview as they publicly attack and malign Christianity, conservative values, and conservative politicians in the classroom. During the 2008 presidential campaign, I visited a number of Wisconsin universities to observe the history, political science, and social studies faculty departments. There were political endorsements for Barack Obama on almost all the faculty office doors and bulletin boards, along with a number of derisive signs against President Bush and Senator McCain. All the college newspapers endorsed Obama with "Obama Hope and Change" symbols plastered throughout the newspapers and campuses. It is sad to think not much has changed; that's the way it was at ASU in the 1970s and still is. It should not surprise us to see that most teachers think in the same political categories and have aligned their curriculum to fit their politically correct education and as the NEA dictates, thus producing cookie-cutter, automaton "teacher think." Once in a while I would find a colleague whose values and worldview disagreed with the left-wing agenda of the NEA, but most were too scared or poorly equipped to fight the NEA-ACLU leviathan. While there were a number of conservative or Republican teachers in the conservative area I taught, they rarely if ever challenged the NEA-WEAC status quo and power establishment. In the Milwaukee and Madison areas, finding a conservative or Republican teacher willing to speak out is next to impossible. In 1988, during the George H. W. Bush–Dukakis presidential campaigns, a number of times I received Democratic propaganda in my teacher's mailbox. I went into the principal's office and asked why this could happen in America, where I explained that, unlike National Socialist Germany, Soviet

Socialist Russia, or Castro Socialist Cuba, we have more than one party. My boss just smiled and said, "The union." How in America did we get to where the NEA-WEAC in socialist style dictates its propaganda in government public schools? How did the NEA-WEAC get in the pocket of the Democratic Party, or should I say how did the Democratic Party get into the pocket of the NEA-WEAC? The answer is Power!

Self-perpetuating scratch my back, I'll scratch your back off the backs of taxpayers power!

Samuel L. Blumenfeld's classic work, *NEA: Trojan Horse In American Education*, states:

> In 1967, the National Education Association declared war on the American people. Its executive secretary proclaimed: "NEA will become a political power second to no other special interest group... NEA will organize this profession from top to bottom into logical operational units that can move swiftly and effectively and with power unmatched by any other organized group in the nation..." Today, that prediction is a reality. The 3.2-million-member NEA is the most politically powerful—and dangerous—organization in the United States with plans not only to control the federal government but also every state legislature in America. Under the guise of "improving education," the teachers are on the march toward total political power with the aim of converting America into a socialist society.

This power came by connecting and interfusing with the Democratic Party. This connection did not happen overnight but was solidified with the influence of the father of modern education, John Dewey. John Dewey was an avowed socialist, the co-author of the *Humanist Manifesto*, and was cited as belonging to fifteen Marxist-front organizations by the Committee on Un-American Activities. Dewey taught the professors who would train America's teachers. Dewey was especially influential as the atheist philosopher of "progressive education." He sought the reconstruction of society through education in which children discovered knowledge for themselves without the restraints of a classical or Christian education. Dewey believed neither the Judeo-Christian biblical worldview nor the study of metaphysics could provide legitimate moral or social values, though secular scientific empiricism could. Dewey and other progressives shifted education from the classical-biblical curriculum to one that emphasized the "social studies" and a more socialist-collectivist system to "socialize the child." He was obsessed with the collective, or the group. He taught, "You can't make socialists out of individualists. Children who know how to think for themselves spoil the harmony of the collective society which is coming, where everyone is interdependent." Rosalie Gordon, writing on Dewey's progressive-socialist education in her book *What's Happened To Our Schools*, states:

> The progressive system has reached all the way down to the lowest grades to prepare the children of America for their role as the collectivists of the future. The group not the individual child is the quintessence of progressivism. The child must always be made to feel part of the group. He must indulge in group thinking and group activity.

And so must the teacher.

When Dewey and other NEA officials visited the Soviet Union in the 1920s, they praised the wonders of Soviet-Socialist education and brought back with them Soviet pedagogic educational styles and methodologies that influenced the teaching of sociology, psychology, and other social sciences in America's public schools throughout the '30s, '40s, and '50s. An excellent history of this development in NEA progressive education can be found in Samuel Blumenfeld's *NEA: Trojan Horse In American Education*, chapter 13, "The Soviet Connection." Matt Gerwitz, in his essay "Dirty Little Secrets: What the NEA Doesn't Want You To Know," writes:

> In 1936, the National Education Association stated the position, from which they've never wavered: "We stand for socializing the individual." The NEA in its Policy For American Education opined: "The major problem of education in our times arises out of the fact that we live in a period of fundamental social change. In the new democracy, education must share in the responsibility of giving purpose and direction to social change... The major function of the school is the social orientation of the individual. Education must operate according to a well-formulated social policy.

Notice the NEA's language of "the new democracy," which would work to change our republic's emphasis on individual God-given rights to create social policy to socialize the individual in collectivist "group thinking." Thus, in public school education today, teachers live within a world of "teacher think," where too many teachers think, speak, and teach within the dictates of the NEA's left-wing, politically correct worldview and values. To not do so or to think or speak out of the party line will bring down the wrath of the NEA-ACLU legal powers that be.

The continued cultural-Marxist undermining of America's Judeo-Christian worldview in education is exemplified by the creation of the 1933 *Humanist Manifesto*, signed by John Dewey and thirty-three other liberal ministers, editors, socialist educators, and cultural Marxists. The Manifesto's worldview rejected biblical-creationism presuppositions that God created the heavens and the earth, and reflected the influences of Darwinian evolution, humanistic psychology, sociology, and the social sciences that were reshaping American education. The *Humanist Manifesto* called for a "redistribution of wealth," and John Dewey, the father of American progressive education and one-time leader of the socialistic League for Industrial Democracy, advocated like Karl Marx for the need for a universal economic socialism where "social control of economic forces are necessary if economic equality is to be realized." By the 1973 publication of the *Humanist Manifesto II*, signed by behavior psychologist B.F. Skinner, Planned Parenthood President Alan F. Guttmacher, National Organization for [Liberal] Women founder Betty Friedan, and many other progressives, socialists, and liberal leaders and educators, the NEA had endorsed its platform and promoted the anti-Judeo-Christian worldview values it espoused. The NEA, ACLU, and secular humanists have worked in tandem to destroy republican Christian education. *The Humanist Review* magazine observed:

> Education is thus a most powerful ally of humanism. What can a theistic Sunday school meeting for an hour once a week and teaching only a fraction of the children do to stem the tide of the five-day program of humanistic teaching?

Paul Blanchard, writing for the *The Humanist* magazine, extols government education by stating:

> I think that the most important factor moving us toward a secular society has been the educational factor. Our schools may not teach Johnny how to read properly, but the fact that Johnny is in school until he is 16 tends toward the elimination of religious superstition. The average American child now acquires a high school education, and this militates against Adam and Eve and all other myths of alleged history. When I was one of the editors of The Nation in the twenties, I wrote an editorial explaining that golf and intelligence were the two primary reasons that men did not attend church. Perhaps today I would say golf and a high school diploma."

Blanchard, like Vladimir Lenin, Roger Baldwin, the ACLU, and the NEA, understood the lasting impact a secular-atheistic public high school education would have on the worldview of America's youth. Professor Chester M. Pierce, M.D., professor of education and psychiatry at Harvard, understood this worldview battle in the public schools when he wrote:

Every child in America entering school at the age of five is mentally ill because he comes to school with certain allegiances to our Founding Fathers, toward our elected officials, toward his parents, toward a belief in a supernatural being, and toward the sovereignty of this nation as a separate entity. It's up to you as teachers to make all these sick children well by creating the international child of the future.

In 1965, the NEA was to be a part of LBJ's socialistic "Great Society," as President Johnson and the NEA teamed up to create the Elementary and Secondary Education Act of 1965, at that time the single largest transfer of federal taxpayers' money to government education. Education has never been the same since. Throughout the '60s and '70s, the NEA decided to join other public-employee unions in creating the Coalition of American Public Employees (CAPE). The CAPE's purpose was to give public employees and Democratic politicians a stranglehold on the taxpayer. The NEA is one of the key players in Democratic Party politics as they endorse the democratic candidates that promise them the most money. From municipalities to counties to state capitals to the election of Jimmy Carter to the White House in 1976, the NEA was essential to Democrat victories. The NEA colluded with President Carter to create the Department of Education in 1979. They promised Carter votes, while Carter promised money and a Federal Department of Education, the long-time dream of the NEA socialists to gain more power beyond state capitals. After the 1976 Carter endorsement, the NEA has been a vociferous backer of every subsequent Democratic presidential nominee. University of Virginia political scientist Larry Sabato once observed, "It's fair to say that the democrats would be nowhere without them." Over these past three decades, the NEA has permeated Democratic politics with money. Literally tens of millions of taxpayer dollars have gone for political gifts and favors. The NEA's political support goes almost exclusively to the Democratic Party. Between 1990 and 2010, 96 percent of NEA candidate and party donations went to Democrats. It is important to note that while I've written mainly about the NEA and WEAC, other corrupt teachers' unions go by their local or state names: for example, the MEA, Michigan Education Association; the NJEA, New Jersey Education Association; the UTLA, United Teachers of Los Angeles; and the New York City teachers who usually go by the name UFT, United Federation of Teachers.

A classic example of the power of teachers' unions to establish socialism in a society is France. Just about when the French people thought the totalitarian proto-communistic ideas of the French Revolution were dying in France, in 1981, socialist Francois Mitterrand won the election for the French presidency. Mitterand's Socialist Party had seventy seats and a true majority. Mitterand appointed the militant socialist Pierre Mauray as his Prime Minister. Mauray's cabinet was made up of socialists and four communists. Mitterand immediately set out to change and transform France's "rupture with capitalism" with a staunch socialistic agenda "to free the workers from age-old oppression and to provide all those who are exploited… with the instruments of their own self-emancipation." Mitterrand's government seized most of France's private banks, socialized eleven large industrial conglomerates, raised the minimum wage, expanded social benefits, raised taxes, and with the help of "the largest occupational bloc of socialists deputies," took control of France's 10,000 private schools, most of them Catholic. What happened in France is what the NEA, its affiliates, and associates have been trying to do for many years in America. Not only do private religious schools, home schools, and alternative schools fly in the face of the NEA's secular progressive agenda, they are competition to their power. Many times in my public school teaching career either at work or at conferences, when I discussed my family's true diversity in sending my children to private Christian schools and public schools and homeschooling them, I was met with incredulous responses of betrayal to the cause, infidelity to public school education, and NEA sound bites like, "Your kids must be lacking in socialization and a solid education." To these I would respond:

> Like the NEA-endorsed Al Gore and Barack Obama, I have sent my kids to a private school. My son and my daughter excelled in all the schools they attended, they have many dear friends, do ballet and soccer, visit museums, design Shakespearean dresses, study film noir, work for Apple, have traveled to London, Rome, Athens, Paris, Florence, Zurich, Anzio and Omaha Beaches, and visited the ruins of Pompeii.

I usually get cut off and can't finish a proud father's litany of my children's "lack of socialization and a poor private and home-schooling educational experience." This is "teacher-union think" at its finest.

What have NEA and other teachers' unions' taxpayers' dollars bought them? Not only the Big Government Department of Education with its cultural-Marxist mandates, but explosive spending at the federal, state, and local levels in education. John Berthold, in his article "NEA: 30 Years of Lobbying Democrats," writes:

> After several decades of massive NEA political spending, this diversity has disappeared from the Democratic Party. Today, any elected Democrat who wishes to move up in the party's ranks realizes he must toe the NEA line on education policy. That means supporting ever-escalating spending, opposing school choice, advocating smaller class size (i.e., hiring more teachers), and blocking all efforts at accountability, such as merit pay. Recognizing the power of the NEA, many Republicans shy away from speaking the truth on these issues as well.

That was, of course, until 2010–11 when Wisconsin Republican Governor Scott Walker, along with a Republican-controlled Assembly and Senate, did not shy away from speaking the truth on the issues of balancing the budget and taking on the Wisconsin teachers' union who were arrogantly ignoring the will of the people of Wisconsin, causing the mobocrats to ascend upon Madison like it was the Bastille of Saint-Antoine.

CHAPTER 14

POWER TO THE PEOPLE
AND THE PROTESTOR

"Viva La Minutemen & Fruit Vendors!"
-Jake Jacobs

"The mob is the mother of tyrants."
-Diogenes

"Socialists cry 'Power to the people,' and raise the
clenched fist as they say it. We all know what they really mean—power over the people, power to the State."
-Margaret Thatcher, Prime Minister of Great Britain

Time magazine called its 2011 Person of the Year "The
Protestor." Time's "Person of the Year Introduction," written by Rick Stengel, was accompanied by a picture of the socialist
clenched fist. Stengel discusses how a sole protestor who set himself
on fire in Tunisia would spark protests that would bring down
dictators in Tunisia, Egypt and Libya and rattle regimes in Syria,
Yemen, and Bahrain. Or that the spirit of dissent would spur
Mexicans to rise up against the terror of drug cartels, Greeks to
march against unaccountable leaders, Americans to occupy public spaces to protest income inequality, and Russians to marshal
themselves against a corrupt autocracy.

Almost as monumental as the minuteman's shot heard around the world at Lexington, Massachusetts, in 1775, a Tunisian fruit vendor's suicide was Time magazine's flame that spread the fires of democracy around the world.

Viva La minutemen and Tunisian Fruit Vendors!

Stengel goes on to describe this international democratic movement:

> Everywhere, it seems, people said they'd had enough. They dissented; they demanded; they did not despair, even when the answers came back in a cloud of tear gas or a hail of bullets. They literally embodied the idea that individual action can bring collective, colossal change. And although it was understood differently in different places, the idea of democracy was present in every gathering. The root of the word democracy is demos, "the people," and the meaning of democracy is "the people rule." And they did, if not at the ballot box, then in the streets. America is a nation conceived in protest, and protest is in some ways the source code for democracy—and evidence of the lack of it.

There's that wonderful word democracy again, with Time magazine telling us it means "the people rule," if not in the ballot box then in the streets. Yes! Time magazine helped me remember my experience during the 2011 Winter Woodstock in Madison, Wisconsin, as tens of thousands of mobocrats, disgruntled with the ballot-box conclusion of 2010, took to the streets threatening bodily harm to republican representatives while shouting, "This is what democracy looks like!" Hmmm... same delusionary dogma, same chant as the "Eat the Rich" Occupy mob.

Time magazine magically mixes all worldwide movements of despair over dictatorships—corrupt autocracy, drug cartels, unaccountable leaders, and income inequality—with the idea of democracy. Hmmm. "Income inequality." Where have we heard that phrase before? And individual action will bring about "collective colossal change." Hmmm. "Collective" and "change." Where have we heard those words before?

Who was Time magazine's Person of the Year in 2008? "Yes-we-can Barack Obama!" We sure got "collective colossal change."

It is not a coincidence that Time magazine writers have chosen those socialistic words and catch phrases as they equate America's Occupy protestors to those in the streets of Cairo and Tunis. Even Tunis and Cairo have their mobocrats, as Daniel J. Flynn writes in his article "Mob Mentality, Mob Rules, We all Lose":

> Shortly after the Western media beatified the Egyptian mob, it ravaged a star CBS correspondent. Shouting "Jew! Jew!" as they sexually brutalized the non-Jewish Lara Logan, the barbarian horde succumbed to the classic mob mentality of dehumanizing outsiders, in this case, women and Jews, to rationalize inhumane acts. Clearly, the mob didn't expel what ails Egypt by deposing Hosni Mubarak.

And the Madison mob called Walker Hitler and Mubarak.

Time magazine's Ivy-League journalists, in typical left-wing subjective manner, have sanitized Occupy's nutty, militant, and

Marxist components while portraying the "Eat the Rich" mob as wise, just, and democratic. You can even buy a copy of Time magazine's new book, *What Is Occupy? Inside the Global Movement*, where their "journalists explore the roots and meaning of the uprising over economic injustice."

Hmmm. "Economic injustice." Where have we heard that socialistic rhetoric before?

Wise and just the "Eat the Rich" movement most definitely is not.

"Democratic" is more fitting, as that is what much of the Occupy movement is about as it defies the rule of law, mocks the Constitution, despises capitalism, demands the property of America's creative and hard-working producers, and ridicules our Republic under God. How silly that the Eat the Rich 99% crowd forgets that their evil 1% created many of the wonderful items that make their life easier and richer today.

The same players, actors, and supporters that I encountered in Madison's "Walker is Hitler" rallies are the same players, actors, and supporters in the "Eat the Rich" rallies staged across America. President Obama, Harry Reid, Nancy Pelosi, Bernie Sanders, and the Democratic Party equated themselves to and supported both movements. Democrats in the millions support both movements. Michael Moore, the Janus-faced, multi-millionaire, agitprop film maker supported both movements; Che Guevara T-shirt-wearing Rage Against the Machine and many rockers supported both movements; Hollywood Lefties supported both movements;

MSNBC's Chris Matthews, Ed Schultz, and Rachel Maddow supported both movements; the NEA, AFL-CIO, SEIU, ACLU, FFRF, LGBT, anarchists, socialists, communists, and millions of young naive college kids and government teachers support and equate to both movements. And so does Time magazine as they write in their Protestor article:

> In the U.S., three acute and overlapping money crises—tanked economy, systemic financial recklessness, gigantic public debt—along with ongoing revelations of double dealing by banks, new state laws making certain public-employee-union demands illegal and the refusal of Congress to consider even slightly higher taxes on the very highest incomes mobilized Occupy Wall Street and its millions of supporters.

America's "overlapping money crisis" was not brought about by the failure of the free-enterprise system or by our republican form of government. Our money crisis was created by the same mob mentality that has plagued mankind from time immemorial. Our Founders' republican worldview and form of government anticipated the mobocrat that covets and steals thy neighbor's goods under the guise of democracy, fairness, social justice, and sharing the wealth. With socialist fists held high, the mobocrats scream out "Power to the people" and "This is what democracy looks like" as they demand that the State take from the people to give to the people.

Eventually you run out of people; eventually you run out of property; eventually you run your republic into the ground and create the democracy our Founders warned us about.

There is no doubt that both the "Walker is Hitler" and "Eat the Rich" mob movements are much, much more than "twin sons of different mothers." They come from the same destructive and deceitful DNA cells that, like cancer, consume the healthy and honest cells around them. Not all protestors believe Governor Scott Walker is Chancellor Adolf Hitler, nor do they want to eat the rich. But unfortunately, many well-intentioned protestors in the crowd do not realize they are involved with a mass-mob mentality that is on the path to the "eve of destruction" in our republic. French social psychologist Gustave Le Bon covers this disturbing "group think-mass mob mentality" in his classic work, *The Crowd: A Study of the Popular Mind*, which was used by Benito Mussolini and Adolf Hitler to learn how to incite a mob.

Le Bon explains: The "convictions of crowds assume those characteristics of blind submission, fierce intolerance, and the need of violent propaganda which are inherent in the religious sentiment." According to Le Bon, the mob thrives on jargon, repetitive slogans, and even tribal drumbeats as a substitute for clear, individual thought. The more dramatic and devoid of logic a chant is, the better it works to rile up a mob: "Given to exaggeration in its feelings, a crowd is only impressed by excessive sentiments. ...To exaggerate ...and never to attempt to prove anything by reasoning is methods of argument well known..."

Did not the many mob signs in Madison say "Scott Walker = Adolf Hitler" and "Walker is a Dick-tator"? Did not the NEA-WEAC, SEIU, AFL-CIO, and ACLU join arm in arm with the crowd in Madison and on Wall Street demanding democracy the mob way? Mobocrats love slogans because, according to Le Bon, "laws of logic have no action on crowds." Le Bon called this thinking the "law of the mental unity of crowds." Mobs, Le Bon says, "are not to be influenced by reasoning, and can only comprehend rough-and-ready association of ideas." If Le Bon was alive today, he could be referring to the NEA and other unions of powerful persuasion and opinion when he describes propaganda slogans and literature that is regurgitated over and over again as they have, according to Le Bon, "manufactured opinions for their readers and supply them with ready-made phrases which dispense them of the trouble of reasoning."

Did not the unreasonable Madtown mobster crowd call Governor Walker over and over again a dictator, Hitler, Mubarak, and Stalin? Did not the Republican representatives need police protection as the unreasonable Democratic mobsters threatened bodily harm and even disturbed the peace of Scott Walker's home and neighborhood? The sad answer to both those questions is yes!

In 2012 and beyond, study the crowd's irrational signs, symbols, and socialistic rhetoric. Observe the 2012 Recall Walker crowd, the 2012 election crowd, and the Occupy crowd as the NEA-WEAC, SEIU, AFL-CIO, ACLU, CPUSA, SPUSA, etc. etc. will use slogans, symbols, signs, and rhetoric that reflect Gustave Le

Bon's brilliant analysis of the mind of "The Crowdocrats," also known as democrats and mobocrats.

You might say, "Hey, wait a minute! You can't call all Democrats mobsters, "crowdocrats," and practitioners of mobocracy!" This is true. I know many nice Democrats, my neighbor lady and some of my teaching colleagues, for example. But far too many Democrats and those of the Democratic establishment have become the crowd, the mob. The Democratic Party of 2012 is not the Democratic Party of my dad. It was fourteen Democratic representatives that left Wisconsin. It was the Democratic Party from the White House to the DNC and beyond that supported and participated with the mob's unreasonable demands on our nation. And it is an overwhelmingly large percentage of Democrats who have joined the mob to harass Republican representatives, while working for their recall, to undo the people's decision to elect Republicans to work within a republican form of government.

In Ann Colter's compelling book, *Demonic: How The Liberal Mob Is Endangering America*, she lucidly writes:

> The Democratic Party is the party of the mob, irrespective of what the mob represents. Democrats activate mobs, coddle mobs, publicize and celebrate mobs—they are the mob. Indeed, the very idea of a "community organizer" is to stir up a mob for some political purpose. "As so frequently happens when a crowd goes wild," historian Erik Durschmied says, "there is always one who shouts louder and thereby appoints himself as their leader." Those are the people we call "elected Democrats." The Democrats' playbook doesn't involve heads on pikes—as

yet—but uses a more insidious means to incite the mob. The twisting of truth, stirring of passions, demonizing of opponents, and relying on propagandistic images in lieu of ideas—these are the earmarks of a mob leader. Over and over again, one finds the Democrats manipulating the mob to gain power. It is official Democratic policy to appeal to the least-informed, weakest-minded members of the public. Their base consists of soccer moms, actresses, felons, MSNBC viewers, aging Red-diaper babies, welfare recipients, and government workers—who can never be laid off.

In typical mobocratic form, MSNBC's Democrat Ed Schultz, when talking to his predominately Democratic audience about the possible election of Republican Scott Brown in Massachusetts, revealed his mobocratic mindset when he stated:

> I tell you what, if I lived in Massachusetts I'd try to vote 10 times. I don't know if they'd let me or not, but I'd try to. Yeah, that's right. I'd cheat to keep these bastards out. I would. 'Cause that's exactly what they are.

This was the same MSNBC Ed Schultz who set up shop in Madison with the Walker-is-Hitler mob and went on a rampage about the evil Republicans and their "bastard" leader Governor Scott Walker.

My experiences with both the "Walker is Hitler" and "Eat the Rich" crowds illustrate on many levels Le Bon's conclusions as slogans and chants described Walker, the republicans, and the rich as Hitler, Stalin, Mubarak, scum, evil, haters, fascist, stupid, vampires, and on and on and on. There was no reasoning with the democratic crowd as the incessant drumming and chanting of, "This is what democracy looks like" proved that the mob is what democracy looks like and why our Founders rejected it so vociferously!

I remember in December 2010, shortly after Republican Scott Walker was chosen by the people of Wisconsin to represent them as the governor of our great state, and while he was attempting to negotiate with the power-hungry Wisconsin teachers' union, there was a protest in England over the Prime Minister's decision to have students pay more for their college education because England, like Wisconsin, was deeply in debt.

Like the "Eat the Rich" and "Walker is Hitler" mob rallies, tens of thousands of college kids, along with anarchists, socialists, communists, and laborites, gathered in Parliament and Trafalgar Squares carrying signs that read "F**K the Fees: Save EMA Free Education," "Tory Pigs," "Marx was right," "Class warfare," "Beer, Pot, Noodles and no Fees," "Free Palestine," "Cardiff UNI Socialist Students," "This is what democracy looks like," and thousands more anarchist, socialist, communist, and union signs and flags that conveyed their demand for "free" money from the people. The famous Winston Churchill statue was defaced and graffitied with "Education for the masses" spray-painted on it. A number of radical Marxists and anarchists, while screaming for revolution in the streets, set fires near the Parliament building. Anarchist-masked, red-revolution-flag-carrying Charlie Gilmour, the son of Pink Floyd's famous multi-millionaire guitar player, David Gilmour, attempted to set fire to the Supreme Court building, hung from a Union Jack flag on the Cenotaph statue honoring Britain's war dead, and while attacking the Prince of Wales and the Duchess of Cornwall yelled with his mobster comrades, "Off with their heads," "Tory scum," and "Give us some money." The English newspaper Telegraph described Gilmour's mobocratic rants and raves this way:

> Shouting slogans such as "you broke the moral law, we are going to break all the laws," the 21-year-old son of the multi-millionaire pop star went on the rampage during a day of extreme violence in central London. Video captured by police officers outside the Houses of Parliament showed Gilmour, from Billingshurst, West Sussex, waving a red flag and shouting political slogans. The judge watched one clip in which he was shouting "Let them eat cake, let them eat cake, they say. We won't eat cake, we will eat fire, ice, and destruction, because we are angry, very f***ing angry." As the clip was shown in court, Gilmour sat in the dock giggling and covering his face with his hands in embarrassment. On another occasion he could be seen urging the crowd to "Storm Parliament" and shouting, "We're going to break all the laws. Arson!"

Charlie Gilmour, the spoiled bourgeois son of privilege and Cambridge University history major, is sadly symbolic of many mobocrats from Athens, Greece to Wall Street, New York and Madison, Wisconsin. Many of the students I talked with at the

"Walker is Stalin" crowd and the "Capitalism is Evil" rallies were students at the University of Wisconsin-Madison where their left-wing education feeds their impressionable young minds with revisionist-Marxist history, where Che Guevara is their hero, V for Vendetta their favorite movie, and Michael "I-hate-capitalism" millionaire Moore is their favorite schlockumentary maker and campus speaker.

As I study and observe the Madison and Occupy movement across America and in Wisconsin, I'm reminded of the wisdom of Aristotle who wrote:

> Young people have exalted notions, because they have not been humbled by life or learned its necessary limitations; moreover, their hopeful disposition makes them think themselves equal to great things ... and that means having exalted notions. They would always rather do noble deeds than useful ones: Their lives are regulated more by moral feeling than by reasoning... all their mistakes are in the direction of doing things excessively and vehemently.

I have to admit that, during my high school and college years in the '70s, too many of my political activities were driven by excessive zealous feelings and not regulated by reasoned discipline. It felt good to feel, talk, and demonstrate for social justice. It felt good to seek a newer and better world and, in many cases, we justified our views of justice by unjustly demanding the property of others and violating the laws of the land. In fact, in 1968, after watching the Summer Olympics where John Carlos and

Tommie Smith wore black gloves and raised their fists in the air in defiance of Olympic protocol, I went to school the next day dressed all in black and wearing a black glove as I went down the hallways at James Madison Junior High School yelling "Freedom for All!" "Civil Rights for All!" My dad did not think it was too funny when I was suspended from school.

I admire passion, but passion in peace, passion with a practical plan, passion that does not attack the police, disturb the public's right to a peaceful neighborhood, defy the law, call Governor Walker Hitler and Stalin and capitalism evil, or call us to eat the rich. Yes, people who do so have a right to assemble peaceably, but not a right to occupy private property and violate federal, state, and city statutes. It's just like the Students for a Democratic Society of the '60s, when many well-intentioned young people were used by radical communists, socialists, and anarchists in their quest to destroy our Republic under God.

Today's Occupy movement is redux 1960s with the same radical players on the stage and, unfortunately, many good-hearted, well-intentioned but naïve young people are being used as pawns in this mobocratic game. Let's not forget what kind of path good intentions can create. I remember my mother always saying to me in my teen years, "Show me your friends and I'll tell you who you are." Her wisdom sounded a lot like Proverbs 13:20: "He who walks with wise men will be wise, but the companion of fools will suffer harm."

Many within the Occupy mob are very young and easily manipulated. What the University of Cambridge's "Charlie Gilmours" and the University of Wisconsin's "Patti Peaceniks" of the world don't understand is that there are very vile and violent people in the world that scour the earth looking for unsuspecting companions and comrades to join them in the cause for "justice" who, under the guise of hating greed, become greedy themselves, and who, with the revolutionary rhetoric of hating injustice, become unjust themselves. That is why Aristotle and our Founders warned that the young are not "discerning hearers" of politics. Their minds are already made up as they theoretically seek an ideal and utopian world. Aristotle reasoned that young adults don't have enough real-world experience nor do they understand the complexities of human nature and political life. That inexperience, coupled with passion and raw emotion, is a natural fit for the mob.

This is not to take away from the legitimate fight for the righteous cause of liberty and justice, but it is to warn zealous youth: "Protestor, beware!" The cause you join today may be with the very enemy of liberty you thought you were fighting against.

Don't let the spontaneous myth fool you. Occupy Wall Street is a movement that has been planned and executed by anarchists, socialists, Marxists, and Big Labor in America for a long time. Follow the money and influence and you find the same characters you found in the "Walker is Hitler" mob, Democratic Socialists of America, IWW, PSL, ACORN, SEIU, NEA, ACLU, CPUSA, SPUSA, the DNC, the Obama administration, the Working

Families Party, the socialist New Party, Tides Foundation, and billionaires like socialist George Soros.

Terresa Monroe-Hamilton writes:

> "Yes, there are evil corporations and evil rich guys like George Soros. There always have been and always will be. But by and large, big companies and the wealthy are what create jobs and prosperity in this country. Without them, you have no America. You have Russia.
>
> So instead of protesting the banks, corporations and feeding the "eat the rich" mantra, Americans should look to the Fed and to the White House and D.C. This is where protests and anger should be leveled, not through a Socialist/Marxist lens that focuses on wealth redistribution and something-for-nothing schemes. Instead of living in the freest nation on earth and having the chance for anyone to succeed, regardless of race, age, religion, sex, or political bent, everyone will equally live in poverty and slavery and the elite will rule over us. That is what Occupy Wall Street accomplishes. It doesn't address the burdens this nation is struggling under; it advances our demise at warp speed."

Sadly, the mob, Obama, and the Democrats advance our republic's demise at warp speed! I am still dumfounded as to why so many Americans are indifferent to the radical groups that comprise so many of the protest movements in America. They were all over the "Walker is Hitler" protests in 2011 and they permeate the Occupy and "Recall Walker" movements as I write this in 2012.

While addressing a gathering of the World Federation of Democratic Youth in Lisbon, Portugal, November 10, 2011, Young Communist League USA (YCLUSA) organizer Lisa Bergmann boasted of communist leadership in the U.S. Occupy movement and their desire to drive the movement to influence the 2012 re-election campaign of President Barack Obama. Here are some alarming parts of her speech:

> Youth in the United States are shouting at the top of their lungs that the U.S. capitalist economic system has failed them... Thousands of youth in the United States are taking to the streets to demand a better world. Inspired by the "Arab Spring" and other youth movements in Europe and Latin America, the Occupy Wall Street Movement began in the heart of the U.S. capitalist system, and has now spread to more than 300 cities in the United States. Occupy is predominantly a youth movement, calling attention to the unprecedented wealth inequalities that exist in our country... While the participants in the Occupy movement are members of a wide variety of groups, they all identify as part of the "99" percent of people who do not have access to the country's wealth. The labor movement in the U.S. has been one of the strongest allies to the Occupy movement. Other participants in the Occupy movement include peace activist groups, veterans, elected officials, immigrant rights groups, and of course the Communist Party and the Young Communist League! The Young Communist League, even though we are in a re-building phase, has participated in Occupy in every city where we exist, and has even initiated the Occupy chapters in some cities.

Leaders of the Young Communist League and leaders of the Communist party have been arrested in Chicago on two separate occasions during police raids on the Occupy movement."

Notice how Bergmann goes on to connect the relationship between her communist cause with youth and labor in their campaign for a socialist-aligned, big-government, job-creation bill sponsored by Congresswoman Jan Schakowsky and President Obama, when she says:

"Also, the networks of student-labor alliances in the country have achieved a new level of coordination and power. I had the privilege of attending the AFL-CIO's "Next Up" conference in September, where 800 young workers and leaders gathered to plot the future of the union movement in the U.S. Student leaders who attended the conference reported winning many victories on university campuses. For example, under the direction of United Students Against Sweatshops, students at over 15 universities nation-wide have built a successful campaign to end their universities' contracts with the food-service provider "Sodexo," because of Sodexo's violations of workers' rights in the U.S. and abroad. The labor movement in general has made dramatic investments in young people over the last period of time. Young people are also leading the fight for job creation. The Young Communist League has been collecting signatures nation-wide in support of President Obama's "American Jobs Act" and Congresswoman Jan Schakowsky's "Emergency Jobs to Restore the American

Dream Act." If passed, these bills would create over 4.2 million new jobs in the U.S. Last week, in the city where I live, the Young Communist League and other youth led a march of 200 people in support of jobs for youth and jobs for all."

Ms. Bergmann goes on to boast of recent growth in the Young Communist League's membership:

"As I mentioned earlier, The Young Communist League is in a period of re-building in the United States, and has been for the last year and a half. We are making good progress. We held 5 YCL schools in the last year, in Los Angeles, New Haven, Chicago, Florida, and Texas. At the schools we taught classes about Marx and Lenin, the labor movement, ending racism, and other topics. Also, hundreds of youth are joining the Young Communist League every month online. Because youth are so disillusioned with capitalism in the U.S. right now, this moment is a huge opportunity for building solidarity with and awareness of countries where socialism or communism exist as the dominant system. This includes Cuba and the growing anti-imperialist governments in Latin America. This past weekend the Communist Party and the YCL held a joint meeting on building solidarity with Cuba and the Cuban five."

Although disappointed with President Obama in some areas, Bergmann and the YCLUSA are firmly committed to Obama and the democrats. To quote Plato's *Republic*, "the birds of a feather flock together." To Bergmann, the communist's job is to force

President Obama to do the things he really wants to but can't. She continues:

> "I will speak briefly about the 2012 elections in the U.S. The election of Obama in 2008 was a tremendous victory for the people of the United States and indeed for people all over the world. The election of our first African-American president has been a huge blow to the entrenched racism in our country. Young people are the reason that Obama won the presidency, as he earned 66 percent of the youth vote. Obama continues to push policies that benefit working-class people in the United States. And Republicans continually block these policies to make Obama look ineffective... the fight for jobs and for real solutions MUST include re-electing Obama in 2012. It is the role of the YCL to emphasize this wherever we go, and to try to push youth in the Occupy movement and elsewhere who do not want to work with any politicians to understand that being absent from the political process is only allowing the ultra-right wing to build power. This is also so that working people can continue to focus on building a viable movement for themselves in the United States that will be in a position to stand in solidarity with working people throughout the world. Angela Davis, when visiting Occupy Wall Street on October 31, said, "It is up to US to build a movement. And it is up to Obama to respond to that movement. But he cannot do it on his own."

Gunrunner for the Marxist Black Panthers in the 1970s, and Communist Professor of History at the University of California

Santa Cruz Angela Davis knows that while the Occupy movement needs their socialist soul brother Barack Obama, their "Comrade and Chief" needs them too.

I spent a significant amount of time on the Marxist focus on America's youth because America's college students are the most vulnerable as they are exposed incessantly to left-wing socialism and communism. This cultural and political war needs to focus on the young and their education. The NEA public school agenda, coupled with left-wing academic indoctrination, is damaging America's children beyond recovery. Constitutional republican education is needed now more than ever before radical democracy destroys America.

Here is Andrew Breitbart's big-government list of organizations, groups, and individuals that support, encourage, or sympathize with the Occupy Wall Street movement. Unfortunately, many of their members are young adults who were indoctrinated by their university professors.

Protestors beware! These are not America's Republic-under-God friends!

The 99%: official list of Occupy Wall Street's supporters, sponsors, and sympathizers:

- Communist Party USA Sources: Communist Party USA, OWS speech, The Daily Caller; American Nazi Party Sources: Media Matters, American Nazi Party, White Honor, Sunshine State News

- Ayatollah Khomeini, Supreme Leader of Iran Sources: The Guardian, Tehran Times, CBS News

- Barack Obama Sources: ABC News, CBS News, ForexTV, NBC New York

- The government of North Korea Sources: Korean Central News Agency (North Korean state-controlled news outlet), The Marxist-Leninist, Wall Street Journal, Times of India

- Louis Farrakhan, Nation of Islam Sources: video statement (starting at 8:28), Black in America, Weasel Zippers, Philadelphia Weekly; Revolutionary Communist Party Sources: Revolutionary Communist Party, Revolution newspaper, in-person appearance

- David Duke Sources: Talking Points Memo, video statement, davidduke.com

- Joe Biden Sources: Talking Points Memo, video statement, Mother Jones

- Hugo Chavez Sources: Mother Jones, Reuters, Examiner.com

- Revolutionary Guards of Iran Sources: Associated Press, FARS News Agency, UPI; Black Panthers (original) Sources: in-person appearance, Occupy Oakland, Oakland Tribune

- Socialist Party USA Sources: Socialist Party USA, IndyMedia, The Daily Caller

- US Border Guard Sources: White Reference, www.usborderguard.com, Gateway Pundit, Just Another Day blog

- Industrial Workers of the World Sources: IWW website iww.org, in-person appearances

- CAIR Sources: in-person appearance, Washington Post, CAIR, CAIR New York

- Nancy Pelosi Sources: Talking Points Memo, video statement, ABC News, The Weekly Standard

- Communist Party of China Sources: People's Daily (Communist Party organ), Reuters, chinataiwan.org, The Telegraph

- Hezbollah Sources: almoqawama.org, almoqawama.org (2), almoqawama.org (3)

- 9/11Truth.org Sources: 911truth.org (1), 911truth.org (2), 911truth.org (3); International Bolshevik Tendency Sources: bolshevik.org, Wire Magazine; Anonymous Sources: Adbusters, The Guardian, video statement

- White Revolution Source: whiterevolution.com

- International Socialist Organization Sources: Socialist Worker, socialistworker.org, in-person appearance

- PressTV (Iranian government outlet) Sources: PressTV, wikipedia

- Marxist Student Union Sources: Marxist Student Union, Big Government, marxiststudentunion.blogspot.com

- Freedom Road Socialist Organization Sources: FightBack News, fightbacknews.org; ANSWER Sources: ANSWER press release, ANSWER website, Xinhua

- Party for Socialism and Liberation Sources: Liberation News (1), pslweb.org, The Daily Free Press, Liberation News (2)

Not only is the so-called 99% Occupy Wall Street movement full of radical supporters, it is full of hypocritical millionaire supporters as well. While attacking the richest 1 percent and income inequality while marching on Rupert Murdoch and David Koch homes, they ignore the massive wealth of left-wing celebrities in their own ranks. In fact, it was their wealth and the wealth of many on Wall Street that contributed millions to Barack Obama's presidential campaign and will do so again in 2012.

But when has consistency been important to left-wing protestors?

Paul Wilson of Newsbusters writes:

> The top 25 richest celebrities supporting Occupy Wall Street, according to the website Celebrity Net Worth, possess a combined net worth of just over $4 billion. That's not surprising. Many of the celebrities supporting Occupy Wall Street seem to be oblivious to the amount of wealth they possess. Comedienne Roseanne Barr (worth $80 million) was quoted quite literally in calling for the heads of the wealthy, declaring:

> "I do say that I am in favor of the return of the guillotine and that is for the worst of the worst of the guilty. I first would allow the guilty bankers to pay, you know, the ability to pay back anything over $100 million [of] personal wealth because I believe in a maximum wage of $100 million. And if they are unable to live on that amount

then they should, you know, go to the re-education camps and if that doesn't help, then being beheaded." Barr inadvertently called for the heads of thirteen celebrities supporting the Occupy Wall Street who make more than $100 million, from singer Miley Cyrus to writer Stephen King. Sometime-singer Yoko Ono (No. 1 on the list, at $500 million) is a descendant of a prominent Japanese banking family. Her late husband John Lennon wrote *Imagine* in a Park Avenue penthouse. She threw in her support for the movement, saying, "John is sending his smile to Occupy Wall Street." Former actress and fitness guru Jane Fonda (worth $120 million), who famously supported communism during the Vietnam War, attacked the wealthy when she threw her support to the Occupiers: Any country that has a very, very small narrow layer of very rich, powerful, privileged people and no middle class, and the rest are just really struggling and some of them not making it, is a country that's not going to be stable. Ranked No. 14 was former Vice President Al Gore (worth $100 million), who is better known for his climate change activism and his patronage of private jets. He has also supported Occupy Wall Street, calling it a "true grassroots movement pointing out the flaws in our system." Even those on the list who didn't make the $100-million mark still have extensive wealth. Liberal actor Alec Baldwin (worth $65 million), a spokesman for Capital One Bank, inveighed against "the bailouts the U.S. government gives major corporations every day" and "the excessive fees forced on customers by certain banks," on the Huffington Post. Wealthy liberal filmmaker Michael Moore (worth $50 million) was further down the list but still had enough money when he paid a million dollars for a luxury car and bought a 10,000-square-foot vacation home. On October 25, Moore was brazen enough to deny that he was a member of the 1 percent on CNN's "Piers Morgan Tonight." (He was later forced to admit that he was a member of the 1 percent.) Discredited former CBS anchor Dan Rather (worth $70 million) decried the influence of "big money" in American society, even in news reporting, saying: "We are living in an age when big money owns everything, including the news." (He may have been referencing liberal donor George Soros's massive funding of journalism.) Some celebrities supporting the Occupy movement do not seem to have a firm grasp of what the movement is about. Rapper Jay-Z (worth $450 million) got in trouble for trying to sell T-shirts to Occupiers without "sharing" the proceeds. Rapper Kanye West (worth $70 million) showed up at the Occupy Wall Street movement wearing gold chains. The attempt of these celebrities to rationalize their own wealth while protesting the wealth of others is astonishing.

Here is a list of the twenty-five richest celebrities supporting the Occupy Movement (Source: Celebrity Net Worth):

1. Yoko Ono - $500 million

2. Jay-Z - $450 million

3. David Letterman - $400 million

4. Stephen King - $400 million (tie)

5. Russell Simmons - $325 million

6. Sean Lennon - $200 million

7. Mike Myers - $175 million

8. George Clooney - $160 million

9. Brad Pitt - $150 million

10. Don King - $150 million (tie)

11. Roger Waters (Pink Floyd) - $145 million

12. Jane Fonda - $120 million

13. Miley Cyrus - $120 million (tie)

14. Al Gore - $100 million

15. Roseanne Barr - $80 million

16. Deepak Chopra - $80 million (tie)

17. Kanye West - $70 million

18. Dan Rather - $70 million (tie)

19. Alec Baldwin - $65 million

20. Matt Damon - $65 million (tie)

21. Tom Morello - $60 million

22. Mia Farrow - $60 million (tie)

23. Katy Perry - $55 million

24. Michael Moore - $50 million

25. Susan Sarandon - $50 million (tie)

TOTAL: $4.1 BILLION

The characters in the "Recall Walker is Hitler" movement and the "Rosanne Barr bring back the guillotine" Occupy crowd are a motley crew of celebrates, communists, cooks, college kids, and kooks whose comradeship is connected to the common cause of an incoherent confusion combined with a cacophony of crazy calls for the collapse of capitalism and advancement of community change, Chicago style. From Madison to Los Angeles and back to New York, the Democratic Party and their mobocrat allies cast Republicans and the rich as crony oligarchs who rule only for the benefit of the rich. Their bourgeois, nouveau-riche hypocrisy does not faze them in the least, as facts only confuse their so-called cause for economic justice and democracy for all.

Let's be honest here.

There are rich Republicans and rich Democrats. And yes, rich Republicans contribute to Republican politicians and rich Democrats contribute to Democratic politicians. And yes, there are greedy Republicans and greedy Democrats.

It is when kernels of truth are distorted into monstrous mantras of lies by the mob to extort money from the people that the republic suffers.

The crux of the issue is wealth and power!

Throughout history there has been a permanent tension between the many poor and the few rich. The socialists and communists in the Madtown-Occupy crowds will remind us it was Karl Marx who called them the unrighteous "haves" versus the righteous "have-nots."

One group is not more virtuous than the other.

The unrighteous poor will always use "the Leader" and the masses to demand their fair share in an unfair world. Benjamin Wiker describes it this way:

> A regime can be torn apart from the side of the poor. A democratic revolution occurs "particularly on account of the wanton behavior of the popular leaders," who, on behalf of the poor, harass "those owning property" and "egg on the multitude against them" and "slander the wealthy in order to be in a position to confiscate their goods.

The few unrighteous rich will always use their money for power and control. Wiker thus states:

> The rich can do a lot of damage precisely because they are rich, and they can buy a revolution in government. Just like the democrats, they can rule tyrannically when they rule by their will rather than to the law.

The virtuous rich and virtuous poor may not be neighbors, but they are not enemies and they do not believe in class warfare as taught by Marx, Marcuse, and Mao and preached by Obama, Pelosi, Reid, and their "Walker is Hitler"/Occupy allies.

Our Founders stressed morality, virtue, and character at all levels of society, as they believed that would create a republic worthy of its citizenry and a citizenry worthy of a republic. It was through the delicate balance of a virtuous republican form of government where mutual respect for each other's human dignity and property would make for a healthy, happy, and safe society.

Public Enemy No. 1 to the Radical Left, the Democratic Party, and the Occupy and Madtown crowds is the greedy rich, the corporate fat cats, and the capitalist crooks. Like the poor and the rich, greed will always be with us. Greed is at all levels and in all economic, political, and social systems and societies. While Jean Jacque Rousseau, Voltaire, Robespierre, Proudhon, Comte, Marx, Freud, Lenin, and company deny the fallen, sinful, and greedy nature of man, our Founders most assuredly did not! They understood the potential wickedness of man's soul and greedy ways as they designed our republican form of government.

Yes, Radical Left, Yes, Occupy mob, Yes, Madtown crowd, there is corporate corruption, Ebenezer greed, and crony capitalism in America and in the world today, but they alone are not the primary reason for this season of your discontent.

The greedy, like the needy, have always been with us in plutocracies, aristocracies, oligarchies, democracies, and dictatorships. It has been rare in history to find righteous rulers who have not let greed guide their minds and let power harden their hearts. However, it is equally true that it has been rare in history to find the needy not demanding wealth from both the greedy and the responsible producers to solve their problems and theoretically bring them heaven here on earth.

The Left, in history by their very nature and identification, have always made republicanism and the rich the bourgeois antagonists in their drama, while they acted as the oppressed, poor, proletariat protagonists and the all-knowing saviors of society.

"Et tu Brute!"

No system is perfect because mankind is not perfect. That is not an excuse for the rich or the poor to oppress, steal, or demand the wages or the property of each other. What America's Founders did in designing our republican political, economic, and social system was to create a "system" that dealt with the realities of a sinful, selfish, and greedy humanity that above all else needed the guidance of God to limit its sinful, selfish, and greedy ways. That truth applied for ALL people—rich, middle class, and poor.

The character in the people that we have is the government that we get.

What the Madtown-Occupy protestors do not realize is that their half-truth proclamations of totalitarian means and measures cannot solve society's problems. To destroy capitalism, to punish the rich, to spread the wealth through coercive means has been tried many, many times before in history, with every attempt leading not to liberty, economic justice, and prosperity for all, but to gulags, bloodshed, and a Napoleon, Lenin, Stalin, Hitler, or Castro to clean up the mess while creating an even greater mess.

Here is a 1979 exchange between Nobel Prize Winner in Economic Science Milton Friedman (unlike Obama he actually did something to win his prize) and Phil Donahue on Capitalist "greed" versus socialist redistribution of wealth. As you read it, imagine you are on Wall Street 2012 and as an Occupier you are interviewing a defender of free enterprise:

> Donahue: When you see around the globe the mal-distribution of wealth, the desperate plight of millions of people in underdeveloped countries, when you see so few haves and so many have-nots, when you see the greed and the concentration of power, did you ever have a moment of doubt about capitalism and whether greed's a good idea to run on?

> Friedman: Well, first of all, tell me, is there some society you know that doesn't run on greed? You think Russia doesn't run on greed? You think China doesn't run on greed? What is greed? Of course none of us are greedy; it's only the other fellow who's greedy.

> The world runs on individuals pursuing their separate interests. The great achievements of civilization have not come from government bureaus. Einstein didn't construct his theory under order from a bureaucrat. Henry Ford didn't revolutionize the automobile indus-try that way. In the only cases in which the masses have escaped from the kind of grinding poverty you're talking about, the only cases in recorded history are where they have had capitalism and largely free trade. If you want to know where the masses are worst off, it's exactly in the kinds of societies that depart from that. So that the

record of history is absolutely crystal clear: that there is no alternative way so far discovered of improving the lot of the ordinary people that can hold a candle to the productive activities that are unleashed by a free enterprise system.

Donahue: But it seems to reward not virtue as much as ability to manipulate the system.

Friedman: And what does reward virtue? You think the communist commissar rewards virtue? You think a Hitler rewards virtue? You think—excuse me, if you will pardon me—do you think American presidents reward virtue? Do they choose their appointees on the basis of the virtue of the people appointed or on the basis of their political clout? Is it really true that political self-interest is nobler somehow than economic self-interest? You know I think you are taking a lot of things for granted. Just tell me where in the world you find these angels who are going to organize society for us. Well, I don't even trust you to do that.

Friedman asks Donahue, "Where in the world [would] you find these angels who are going to organize society for us?" From Rousseau's "General Will" to Robespierre's "Committee of Public Safety" to Karl Marx's "Dictatorship of the Proletariat" or the "Democracy" of Madtown and Occupy, the angels of our deliverance in reality become the demons of our demise.

As stated earlier, the poor and the rich and the greedy you will always have with you, but what about the middle class?

I noticed at the "Walker is Hitler" and Occupy "Days of Rage" rallies that there were a number of signs not only calling for class warfare and the eradication of capitalism, but also saying that corporate greed was killing the middle class.

Like Friedman told Donahue, "It's only the other fellow who's greedy." The Occupy Radical Left ignores its own greed as they call for more and more confiscation of other citizens' wealth and property. They create a mythological 99-percent-good guy with a 1-percent-greedy bad guy. What they don't want to admit is that <u>forty-nine percent of U.S. households pay no federal income tax at all</u>, and their guy Obama gave more of our money to the 49 percent nontaxpayers. Socialism for the 49 percent works! No wonder they call the socialist town of San Francisco "the 49ers!" The Radical Left loves our highly progressive U.S. tax system and wants to make it more progressive and punitive. The top 10 percent of workers pay 70 percent of federal income taxes. Last year, the top 1 percent of income earners paid 39 percent of all federal income taxes, while the bottom 50 percent paid only 3 percent.

Much more than corporate greed hurting the middle class is the fact that federal government greed and spending is also hurting the middle class and destroying our republican way of life. While texting and talking on their corporate Apple phones, taking pictures on their corporate Canon cameras, wearing corporate Gap clothes, and organizing through corporate Facebook, the Occupy socialist crowd calls for the collapse of capitalism and the end of corporations through government coercion and control. What the Occupy big-government lovers don't realize is that history teaches us that "a government that is big enough to give you all you want is big enough to take it all away."

Our Founders did not gather their wisdom from a world of slogans and signs where demagogues reinforced the mob's group-think with clichés that demanded something for nothing from responsible citizens. As much as our Founders feared big government, they equally feared the mob being manipulated by power-hungry Machiavellian charlatans. That is why our Founders' living in the real world of haves and have-nots did not create a direct democratic government of the have-nots using the government to steal from the haves. They created a limited republican government where all citizens were to be protected from any class—rich, middle, or poor—harming each other.

Our Founders believed that a free-enterprise system, with limited government involvement in the marketplace, would be the most conducive for job creation and economic and social prosperity. To them, the government's primary purpose was not to create jobs, because to do so would enslave more citizens with higher taxation, thus creating a dependency state where citizens on the public government dole would demand more from the private sector citizens. This is happening today!

The "dependency state" is socialism, and Obama, the Democratic Party, and the Madtown-Occupy crowds adore it.

Our Founders adamantly believed that the government's primary function was to protect the market from unfair play. The government was not to be a player in the marketplace but a referee allowing for equality of opportunity to participate in the market if one desired to do so. This does not mean that our Founders created a government that does not implement "safety nets" for those legitimately in need. But it does mean that a Marxist "cradle to grave" society was the furthest thing from our Founders' limited government minds. Thomas G. West, in his brilliant book *Vindicating the Founders*, writes:

> "Their [Founders] property rights and welfare policies, which are often scorned today for their supposed indifference to the poor, were arguably more just and compassionate than ours."

To our Founders the middle class was the key to a flourishing, stabilized society. Like most of the rich, the middle class believes that hard work should be rewarded. Since they own property they are willing to defend property rights and to fight unreasonable taxation to redistribute the wealth. But while the middle class defends property rights, they also do not see the rich as necessarily more virtuous workers or better qualified to hold political power than anyone else. Our free-enterprise, republican form of government has created the most prosperous middle class in the history of the world, and it is no coincidence that many of our finest citizens have come from the middle class, as they are self-reliant, independent, and hardworking.

Many hardworking, middle-class workers in Wisconsin were appalled during the "Walker is Hitler" rallies as they saw thousands and thousands of hooky-playing teachers not teaching, and hooky-playing students not learning, while mobocratic citizens were demanding more money at their expense. At the rallies I saw Republican signs that said, "I defend Governor Walker on the weekend because I'm too busy working to pay for your demands!" and "We protest on Saturdays because we are too busy working M–F paying for Union greed."

These signs reflect the American middle-class work ethic and worldview that would not occupy Wall Street and Madtown with socialistic sloganeering for spreading the wealth and growing the government off the backs of hardworking Americans.

Jake at the *Occupy Madison* rally with a V for Vendetta protestor. In the book and movie *V for Vendetta*, Christians and Conservatives are portrayed as Nazis

CHAPTER 15

TEA PARTY REPUBLICANISM VS. OCCUPY MOBOCRACY

"I am in favor of the return of the guillotine… they should, you know, go to the re-education camps and if that doesn't help, then being beheaded."
-Rosanne Barr, Occupy movie star

"Eat the Rich before they eat you."
-Christy C. Road, Occupy poster maker

"They are pretty much, as far as I can tell, hooligans and working outside the law. Tea Party people are respectful of the law. We do not trash anything. We respect other people's property. We are just interested in keeping our freedoms."
-Russ Colby, Tea Party activist

Another myth perpetuated by the elite left-wing media is the so-called moral equivalency of the Occupy movement to the Tea Party movement. Talk about an Orwellian perversion of reality!

The Tea Party stands for limited government and limited taxes, and proudly defends our constitutional Republic under God. The Occupy movement stands for bigger government and unlimited taxes and constantly ignores, attacks, and denigrates our wonderful Constitution, calling for democracy not republicanism. The Tea Party trusts in God, not government, while the Occupiers trust in big-democratic government, not God. The Tea Party not only loves to quote America's Founders, but they actually understand the quotes they use and how our Founders designed a republican form of government. The Occupiers are more at home with Marx's *Manifesto* and Marcuse's *Repressive Toleration* than with *The Federalist Papers* and Paine's *Common Sense*. The Tea Partiers do cling to their guns and God while the Occupiers cling to bigger government and utopian illusions. The Occupiers have illegally occupied private property, desecrated public parks, shut down private ports, and battled with police across America from New York to Atlanta, Houston, Seattle, Los Angles, and Oakland. Tea Partiers clean up after themselves and do not defecate on the American flag, wear Che Guevara T-Shirts, fly communist flags, or call for revolution in the streets and the end of capitalism while attacking police. While Tea Partiers' signs and posters reflect clear thinking, love of country, and constitutionalism, the Occupiers' posters are full of vitriolic verbiage of hatred for capitalism, love of class warfare, and violence against the prosperous. Occupy symbolism and signs are full of socialistic slogans and Marxist maxims, while Tea Party signs and symbolism reflect republican virtue and traditional values.

Aaron Klein very astutely observes, in Andrew Breitbart's Big Government blog, the anti-American Marxist elements in the Occupy mobocrat movement when he writes:

> The deployment of Occupy flash mobs could provide the anti-Wall Street movement with a tactical advantage. Occupy mobs appearing at sites without warning could damper the planning of counter-measures by cit-

ies, citizens, and law enforcement." It's helpful here to draw a distinction between optimistic, generous, youth-energized movements demanding an end to corruption while wrongly working outside the framework of the law (as with Occupy) and another, less-visible crew: the intellectual grandchildren of the Soviet ideologues of the mid-twentieth century. It's hard to believe that, two decades after the Soviet Union blew up and expired, there still exist bands of self-described deep thinkers who want one more chance to prove that Marx, Engels, Feuerbach, Lenin, Papa Stalin, and that charmer Mao were on the right track to solving the biggest human dilemma: how can we all get along with each other in a cosmopolitan society. History proves, to borrow one of their phrases, that heirs to Eurasian Marxism are not fussy about means to ends. Stalin killed 20 million of his own citizens; Mao actually killed at least 70 million Chinese people, both Han and "Little Nationalities." These are unthinkable numbers, mainstays of that last century we managed to escape in the hope that this one would turn out better. Normal citizens are astounded to see gray-haired vestiges of that tradition hand in hand these days with teenagers and college students, kids who clearly have no idea what a mess the Marxists made of practical life—and how bitterly corrupt the party leaders inevitably became. It's an eye-opener, therefore, to learn that Obama and Ayers also channeled Woods Fund money to a major Saul Alinsky-based training outfit, the Midwest Academy, whose founder, Heather Booth, has recently been advising unions on how to utilize the economic crisis. An arm of Midwest Academy, Citizen

Action of Wisconsin, was one of the main orchestrators of last February's protests against Governor Scott Walker. Those protests seemed to be the domestic litmus test for Occupy. If Occupy can simmer along for a few months, and all signs indicate that it can, the most ambitious escalation seems set to coincide with major NATO and G8 summits in Chicago next May, when world leaders convene to focus on global economic issues. A gilt-edged list of radical groups, including those behind the 1999 WTO riots, has already petitioned the city for permits to demonstrate. It's the perfect storm for Occupy chaos, for nudging closer to the ultimate goal of "fundamentally transforming"–read: overthrowing–"the American system."

Notice how Klein points out the radical Obama, Ayers, Alinsky, Socialist-Marxist connection to not only the Occupy movement but to the "Walker is Hitler" movement in Wisconsin. Naïve democratic protestors beware! Tea Partiers are lovers of Christianity and are true sons of liberty and daughters of the American Revolution, while Occupiers are children of the Enlightenment, the French Revolution, and its mobocratic legacy of terror.

The Occupiers are usually educated by politically correct, left-wing professors who highlight America's so-called enlightened roots while denigrating or denying our Christian heritage and republican form of government under God. As discussed in an earlier chapter on who won the textbooks, these same professors write America's textbooks for our government schools' kindergarten through college level.

These textbooks permeate with an evolutionary and enlightened worldview value system at the expense of historical truth and context in relationship to Christianity's profound impact in western civilization. While there are hundreds of examples of this bias, let me give you just a few illustrations of this "enlightenment indoctrination" in our government textbooks. In Prentice Hall's 2007 world history textbook's unit on the "Scientific Revolution," there is not one mention of the great contribution the Christian worldview and faith had on Kepler, Tycho Brache, Copernicus, Galileo, and Newton. Students are not taught that Newton wrote more material on his Christian faith than he did on math and physics. On their unit on the "Campaign Against Slavery," all the credit is given to "enlightenment thinkers" while there is no mention whatsoever of the passionate evangelical Christian William Wilberforce, who was the key player in the campaign against slavery. To not mention Wilberforce's contribution to the ending of slavery would be like not mentioning Thomas Jefferson's contribution to the Declaration of Independence. In like manner, most textbooks fail to mention the significant contribution Christianity played in the abolition movements in both Britain and the United States while the Enlightenment is given all the credit.

Related to academia's affinity towards and participation in the Occupy movement is academia's distortion of the portrayal of the intellectual origin of the American Revolution. In Prentice Hall's world history textbook, they titled Chapter 5 "The Enlightenment and The American Revolution," with the words "enlightened," "enlightenment," "enlightenment thinkers," and "enlightenment ideas" being mentioned over forty times as the worldview behind the American Revolution. In typical politically correct fashion there is not one mention of "Christian," "Christianity," or "Christian ideas" being behind the American Revolution.

This politically correct cultural Marxism is so prevalent in academia today that my Ph.D. dissertation, titled "The Influence of Biblical Ideas and Principles on Early American Republicanism and History," was initially rejected by the Arizona Department of Education because of their bogus claim it was a "violation of church and state." Knowing my God-given First Amendment right of freedom of speech and press, I fought the Arizona Department of Education and won, earning Arizona state college credit for my Ph.D.

As with the comparison of the Occupy movement to the Tea Party movement, government academia equates the spirit and worldview of the French Revolution to the American Revolution.

Nothing could be further from the truth. The "democratic" French Revolution despised authentic republicanism, French tradition, Christianity, the rule of law, and due process. With enlightened ideas from Jean Jacque Rousseau's General Will, where one was "forced to be free" by the dictatorial control of an "Enlightened elite," French Revolutionary mobster Maximilien Robespierre and his euphemistically called "Committee of Public Safety" were responsible for the slaughter of tens of thousands of people. Not wanting to be held accountable to the Judeo-Christian

God, YAHWEH, the Supreme Judge of the World (see the last chapter of America's Declaration of Independence), the French mobocrats outlawed Christianity, even going so far as to change the book of Genesis' seven-day week with a pagan ten-day week. They replaced Jesus with the "Goddess of Reason" as they paraded an ex-nun-turned-prostitute throughout the streets of Paris, celebrating a pagan festival at the Cathedral of Notre Dame where they worshiped man's mind or reason over God and His revelation in the Scriptures.

Unlike French mobocrats, America's Founders believed that American citizens were made in the image of God—thus equal, free, and due their due process by the government. In stark contrast, French mobster revolutionaries desired to create in Frankensteinian fashion a "new creature," a new man who would shape a utopian socialistic society where he would produce heaven on earth without God, and if you disagreed with their monster, the mobster would proceed to use the "National razor" without the love of God, the rule of law, and due process.

It was the guillotine over God and democracy over republicanism.

In contrast to the French bloody reign of terror and anarchy, the American War for Independence was predicated on love of God, respect for life, and the rule of law. Drawing on centuries of Judeo-Christian legal thought, our Founders painstakingly pleaded with England's king to live up to his legal covenant obligation with his citizens. When you study the Declaration of Independence you do not read bloodthirsty "revolution" and the utopian "re-creation of man"; rather, you see the American mind and the desire to be free from the tyranny of big government.

Unlike the democratic-mobocrats of France, the Christian republicans of America had a tempered and measured call to arms due to their Christian ethic, which taught them a respect for life and love of liberty. The same analogy applies to republican Tea Party patriotism in contrast to anti-American Occupy socialism. The French Revolution is the true progenitor of the Occupy movement, as citizens storm American streets arm in arm with revolutionary radicals demanding the annihilation of capitalism and the eating of the rich, while Tea Partiers call for love of God and country and the restoration of constitutional republicanism.

While they both have a distrust of greedy and corrupt crony capitalists, the Occupiers call for more rules, more regulations, more taxation, more bureaucrats, more czars, and more government to solve our problems, not admitting that it was the government that created the problems in the first place! Tea Partiers are the true patriots as they do not join in comradeship with those who call for the eradication of capitalism and our republican form of government.

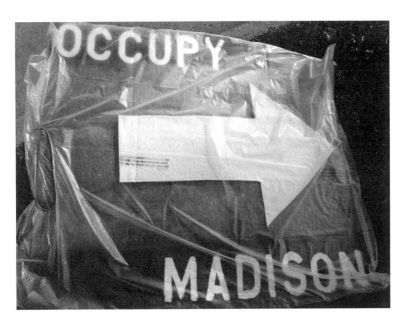

CHAPTER 16

WISCONSIN'S GOVERNOR & REPUBLICAN REPRESENTATIVES STAY THE COURSE FOR THE PEOPLE

"What beats 14 Democratic runners? 1 Republican Walker"
Counter "Walker is Hitler" Slogan

"If he comes out on top in a special election, he is a right wing political star. If he loses, he is a political martyr, but still a star. What Walker represents—the idea behind his policies—cannot be killed even if he is temporarily removed from office."
-Governors Journal on Governor Walker's Recall

In 2009, when I heard Democratic House Speaker Nancy Pelosi characterize the opponents of Obamacare (the trillion-dollar, she-did-not-read-and-needed-to-pass-it-"to-know-what-was-in-it-bill") as swastika-carrying, Astroturf, rich folk I was puzzled. I had previously gone to a number of town hall meetings in Wisconsin where I engaged with numerous ordinary people from all walks of life. They were not Nazis but citizens who were concerned about Obamacare and the record-breaking spending being done by the Democratically controlled Congress. Around the same time I heard of a growing national movement of citizens called "The Tea Party." Hearing MSNBC and Democratic members of Congress calling the citizens attending these Tea Parties "tea-baggers," "radicals," and "brown shirts," I decided to check out the local Appleton Tea Party event being held on tax day, April 15, 2009. As I was walking around watching and talking to the people there, I noticed that there were no "Nazis" there but ordinary middle-America citizens frustrated with the Democratic Congress and the Democratic President Barack Obama breaking their promise to balance the budget while taxing and spending at historic and record-breaking levels. Before I knew it I was asked to speak and got the crowd so enthused about our constitutional republic that I have become a regular speaker at Tea Party events throughout Wisconsin. What surprised many in the audience was that I was a public school teacher who thought independently of the all-powerful NEA-WEAC, and that I did not fall into the politically correct "union teacher think" mindset that supported the agenda of the radical left-wing NEA, WEAC, and AFTW (American Federation of Teachers of Wisconsin).

During the NEA-WEAC and AFTW's 2011 winter of discontent over Governor Walker's campaign promise to stop spending money we didn't have, someone who heard me at a Tea Party contacted Fox & Friends, letting them know there was a teacher in Wisconsin who was publicly defending Governor Walker. When Fox & Friends called my home on that cold February Saturday morning and asked me to speak on the Governor's behalf at the

Capitol the following Sunday, I said to them, "Do you know what you're asking? My name will be worse than mud with my colleagues and my life will never be the same." After I finished teaching my Saturday college class, I came home, called Fox News in New York, and said, "I'll do it." My name soon became worse than mud in some circles and my life has not been the same.

However, what I experienced was nothing compared to what Governor Scott Walker and our brave Republican representatives experienced. From vile name-calling, ugly characterizations, blatant-lying slander, to the disturbing of their and their families' peace and threats of bodily harm, the Democratic and union mob machine continues its war on Walker and on our Republic under God. The official Governors Journal selected Scott Walker as "Governor of the Year in 2011" and rightfully so. When Scott Walker ran for Governor in 2010 he knew Wisconsin was in a mess due to a Democratic governor who, along with a Democratic majority like Obama and his Democratic majority, had spent billions of dollars Wisconsinites did not have while breaking promise after promise of fiscal responsibility. Governors Journal writes of the fiscal irresponsibility that governors across America had to face in 2011:

> Nearly every governor, regardless of party, began the year saying the current path of expensive pension and benefit packages for public employees is unsustainable.

Governors across America from Nevada, Idaho, Indiana, Florida, New York, New Jersey to Wisconsin are trying to find ways to fight the political stronghold teachers' unions have on state budgets. In an interview with ABC News's Diane Sawyer, New Jersey Governor Chris Christie said:

> I believe the teachers in New Jersey in the main are wonderful public servants that care deeply. But their union, their union are a group of political thugs.

While admiring the dedication of public school teachers in New Jersey, Governor Christie understands the thug-nature of teachers' unions in America. Governors Journal's runner-up for Governor of the Year 2011, Democratic Governor Andrew Cuomo, has had to deal with New York public union's political thugs who are suing Cuomo and the state of New York after they refused to negotiate on benefits concessions so Cuomo could attempt to balance New York's budget deficit. We saw that union political "thuggery" on display in Wisconsin in 2011 and still do as WEAC refuses to listen to the voters of Wisconsin as they wage war on Wisconsin citizens and the Governor, even as Governor Walker and the Republicans in Madison have saved millions of dollars for Wisconsin taxpayers.

Unlike the union myth that is out there, Scott Walker did not hide his agenda. Walker was straightforward about the stranglehold that WEAC and other public unions have had on Wisconsin taxpayers. He knew how nice we had it in the public sector compared to many of our friends in the private sector. If you study WEAC and their various union literature pieces shoved in Wisconsin public school teachers' mailboxes throughout the state in 2010, you will see their concern over Scott Walker's "anti-Union agenda." Here are a few examples from WEAC's 2010 election literature used to educate public school teachers on WEAC concerns over Walker's anti-collective bargaining, anti-retirement agenda. They quote from the June 17, 2010, Milwaukee Journal Sentinel on WRS retirement:

> One of Walker's major campaign issues is to require all public employees to pay the Employee share of the pension contribution. This would mean a reduction in take-home pay of about 6.5%. "Milwaukee County Executive Scott Walker said Thursday if elected governor he would save $176 million per year by requiring state employees to contribute toward their pensions."

WEAC then states:

> Currently your employer pays both the employer's and employee's share of the WRS contribution and Mayor Barrett has not promoted legislation that would require public employees to pay the Employee share of the WRS contribution. Instead he has demonstrated a belief that any such changes should occur through the local collective bargaining process.

WEAC understood what Scott Walker's agenda was about. They heard his campaign speeches and read his views on collective bargaining and union control over Wisconsin citizens. Mobocrats create myth in an attempt to fool the citizens.

Here's another WEAC concern over health care and "your right to bargain over your health insurance carrier and plan," as quoted in the August 29, 2010, Milwaukee Journal Sentinel:

> Walker supports a bill that would take away the right of unions to negotiate health care benefits. Ryan Murray, Campaign Policy Advisor for Walker, said, "The way the proposal would work is we would take the choice out of the collective bargaining process."

The WEAC literature goes on to encourage teachers to vote for pro-public union candidate Tom Barrett on November 2, 2010, because he states in a WEAC interview on May 15, 2010:

> I believe in collective bargaining.

The WEAC literature goes on to say:

> Barrett opposes legislation that would take school employees' voice out of the decision-making over health care by allowing school boards to unilaterally change employees' health care coverage plan providers.

This kind of WEAC political and educational material was in my mailbox and Wisconsin's public school teachers' mailboxes throughout the fall of 2010. When teachers tell the press they did not know Walker's agenda until after the election, they are either being disingenuous or they did not bother to read their own union's warnings of Walker's attack on collective bargaining and the costs they would incur if he was elected.

Governors Journal challenges the WEAC myth when it states:

It is not accurate to say Scott Walker launched an unannounced attack on public employees. For decades, state and local government leaders have complained about government employee unions: Collective bargaining, growing benefit packages, under-funded pension systems, and binding arbitration. The warning siren had howled.

Yes! "The warning siren had howled" as an overwhelming majority of Wisconsinites fairly and legitimately elected Republican Scott Walker and a Republican majority (yes, mobocrats, I did say MAJORITY!) in both the Senate and the Assembly. They acted on the will of the people through a republican form of government, and the democratic-mobocratic minority declared war on Wisconsin, and began an illegitimate offensive campaign of blitzkrieg propaganda dive-bombing with Big Bertha guns from MSNBC's "I'd cheat" Ed Schultz, whining Rachel Maddow, socialist-fist screaming AFL-CIO Richard Trumka, and history-twisting Michael Moore, to blame the white-guy Jesse Jackson or Tony "Monk" Shalhoub, and many, many more celebrities perpetuating myth after myth and lie after lie. Even the socialist movie star Susan Sarandon joined the mob in Madison echoing her performance in the "classic" 2000 documentary, *This Is What Democracy Looks Like*, which depicts the 1999 Seattle WTO mobocrat revolution where the likes of communist-loving, Rage Against The Machine declares war on capitalism while going wild in the streets in the style of Lenin, Stalin, Castro, Ayers, and Dohrn.

It is not surprising, as stated earlier, that these "big guns" were also Occupiers on Wall Street. Same gig, same mob, same cause.

These "big gun" tactics were the reason I had been at odds with the Wisconsin teachers' union for years. They not only advocated big-government, left-wing values I disagreed with, but they had through collective bargaining monopolized and manipulated the government workforce. What many teachers and mobocrats refuse to see is that union negotiations operate differently in the private sector from in the government sector. Private unions bargain within a competitive free-enterprise system that has profit as the key source of negotiating wage determination.

While collective bargaining sounds like a "just" labor practice in the public sector, it is, according to David J. Schnarsky of Appleton, Wisconsin:

> A flawed process that ties the hands of school district decision-makers. First, in the private sector, there's a shared concern about jobs and the health of the company that prevents union employees from excessive demands for benefits. In the public sector, no such inhibition exists. Public employee unions negotiate their pay and benefits with elected officials who aren't paying their salaries. The money is coming from taxes that, in theory, can be continuously raised to meet the cost of benefits and there's no spending limit. It's truly a flawed process.

In the private sector, competition from other businesses moderates reasonable wage demands. No such competition exists in government schools (no wonder teachers' unions hate vouchers and related educational alternatives—it threatens their monopoly), and no profits exist to negotiate with; therefore, when government unions demand more tax dollars, they put private citizens at odds with public service. When government unions strike, they deny services paid for by the citizens such as the education of our children. This is why I and millions of Wisconsinites were disgusted with the teachers' blue-flu strike that closed down a number of Wisconsin schools, as it was illegal, immoral, and at our expense. This is also why Democrat FDR, while giving unions extensive power to collectively bargain in the private sector, thought that collective bargaining in the public sector was "unthinkable and intolerable." As it is!

Unlike what I saw in Madison with Obama's mobster ally AFL-CIO President Richard Trumka who, with socialist "blue fist" held high called for war on Walker, The Heritage Foundation tells us that in:

> 1955, George Meany, then-president of the AFL-CIO, said: 'It is impossible to bargain collectively with the government.' In 1959, the AFL-CIO Executive Council declared, "In terms of accepted collective bargaining procedures, government workers have no right beyond the authority to petition Congress—a right available to every citizen."

Governor of the Year 2011 Scott Walker is rightfully reforming collective bargaining abuse in Wisconsin. Before his bold move to take on the monopolizing WEAC and AFT-Wisconsin, they had too much control over our budgets and taxes. Under WEAC's influence, taxes continually went up, and WEAC filled its coffers while school boards were at their mercy. For decades

WEAC, through political hardballing, was able to get exorbitant above-market compensation for their members. In the twenty-eight non-right-to-work states, teachers' unions are able to force government teachers to pay union dues.

Not anymore in Wisconsin, thanks to Governor Walker!

WEAC had the power to elect the management they negotiated with, and they put millions of dollars into Democratic candidates' pockets who promised them more goodies, perks, and benefits from the hardworking taxpayers of Wisconsin. Governor Walker and our Republican representatives have helped restore voter control over the spending of their money. Voters now have the power to approve any wage increase beyond inflation.

What many teachers and union mobsters are unwilling to admit is that fighting public sector unions is a proud American tradition. While Wisconsin union history is mandated in Wisconsin schools, teachers rarely cover in a positive light the fight to curb public union power abuse. Rarely do they differentiate between public and private unions.

Not only did Democrat FDR think public unions were "unthinkable and intolerable," but Republicans Calvin Coolidge and Ronald Reagan would not tolerate their unthinkable mobocratic actions. In 1919, when the Boston police force went on strike causing looting in the streets of Boston, Governor Calvin Coolidge broke the strike declaring, "There is not a right to strike against the public safety of anybody, anywhere, anytime." The citizens of Massachusetts loved him for his bold move, propelling him to the White House. In 1981, when PATCO called for an air traffic controller strike, President Reagan declared their strike was illegal and a "peril to national safety" and ordered them back to work in forty-eight hours. They continued to defy the law and President Reagan legally fired 11,345 illegal strikers.

In 2011, a forty-three-year-old Republican governor responded to the people of Wisconsin's call to get out of debt, balance the budget, not raise taxes, and stop the unfair play and monopolizing of public sector unions. School districts across the state of Wisconsin are elated over the freedom they now have to conduct business without the intimidation and restrictions of WEAC and AFT. WEA Trust Health Insurance had been ripping off taxpayers and school districts for years as they used collective bargaining to deny districts the opportunity to shop for better deals. Now that school boards have the freedom to seek alternative health care providers in the open market, hundreds of thousands and millions of dollars are being saved by school districts throughout the state of Wisconsin. Ashland, Appleton, Baraboo, Dodgeland, Edgerton, Elmbrook, Hartland, Hudson, Kaukauna, Kimberly, Manitowoc, Marshfield, Mequon-Thiensville, Pittsville, Racine, and Wauwatosa are but a few of the school districts lauding Governor Walker and our republican representatives who, like Calvin Coolidge and Ronald Reagan, stood firm with the courage of their convictions, knowing that the power of public sector unions was "unthinkable and intolerable" and needed to be curtailed.

Even Governor Walker's Democratic opponent in 2010, Tom Barrett, has seen the light in 2012 on the intolerable abuse of public sector unions in Wisconsin. As Milwaukee's Democratic mayor, Barrett has taken a "right-Republican" turn on public union benefits as he used Governor Walker's reforms to save the taxpayers $25 million a year. Barrett now believes Governor Walker didn't go far enough because the reforms excluded firefighters and police who were receiving what he called "Cadillac benefits." Hopefully more Democrats will see the error of their ways and join common-sense Republicans and Wisconsinites in stopping the spending of other people's money and money we don't have.

Unfortunately, the madness in Madtown, Wisconsin, is not over as the Democrats or mobocrats continue to pursue a scorched-earth, "Recall Walker is Hitler" policy full of distorted data, perverted propaganda, and *ad hominem* character assassinations of teachers, citizens, and politicians who dare to confront their controlling ways.

It has gotten so bad that Wisconsin fourth grade public school students are being indoctrinated with anti-Walker songs sung in the capitol building in Bob Dylan-Pete Seeger style. The Socialist Solidarity Singers sing protest songs in Madison's capitol rotunda every weekday. One of their chosen songs is Woody Guthrie's, "I Hate the Song 'God Bless America'-This Land is My Land," with a few new lines added at the end that include the words "Scott Walker will never push us out! This house was made for you and me." The fourth graders' teacher thought it was charming and cute until he realized it was being videotaped and could cause Wisconsin citizens to wonder why their tax dollars are being used to indoctrinate young minds to hate Wisconsin's Governor of the Year. "Teacher WEAC think" at its finest.

Governor Walker and Wisconsin citizens have to endure pro-government labor union protestors showing up at every one of his public appearances. These ubiquitous unionists are a constant presence in the rotunda of Madison's capitol. During the lighting of the capitol Christmas tree (Thank you, Governor Walker and Representative Steinke, for standing up to the ACLU and FFRF and calling the Christmas tree what it is—a Christmas tree), a few dozen "Walker is Hitler" mobsters were on hand displaying Nazi salutes as Walker began to speak. Republican State Senator Alberta Darling wrote this on her Facebook page:

> In addition to turning their backs on not just Scott Walker, but also some of our brave veterans, protes-tors thought it was amusing to give a Nazi salute at a Christmas tree-lighting ceremony. Just disgusting.

Disgusting indeed. A relevant digression is in order here.

During my many travels to Europe I saw "Bush is Hitler" post-ers, signs, graffiti, and T-shirts plastered all over shops and on high school and college kids. While in Athens, Greece, I noticed that besides the popular "Bush is Hitler" paraphernalia, the top-selling item was the communist "Butcher of LA Cabana Prison"/Castro's right-hand executioner Che Guevara's image on T-shirts, flags, and coffee mugs. All over Greece I saw communist, socialist, and union symbolism displayed in unity, as comrades in arms demanding more money from the government. The problem with Greece, like Wisconsin, is that the government in office before Scott Walker had run out of other people's money. Under the stewardship of the Papandreou family and socialists in government, they spent all the capital they could steal from their fellow Greeks, and when that ran out they started borrowing, and when that ran out, as they did in Madison, they demanded more. Greek union mobsters are beneficiaries of socialist policies, as Greek union members have become underworked and overpaid and have retirement plans much greater than most private-sector Greeks.

Remember our earlier discussion about Greece being the birthplace of democracy? It never worked there for liberty and it still doesn't work, as hundreds of thousands of mobocratic Greeks storm the streets and attack police while screaming, "This is what democracy looks like" and "Show me the money!" When the mob is done demanding money and democracy in the streets, they go to the ballot box and vote in huge socialist-communist-union blocs to obtain benefits for themselves. This sad direction of European socialistic democracy is following the prophetic script of Friedrich von Hayek's classic work, *The Road To Serfdom*. If the chaos continues in Greece and other parts of Europe, the next step will be martial law and suspension of elections.

Remember how our Founders studied Greece's democracy and knew it was mobocracy and despotism? It has been said that

Benjamin Franklin spoke the following words as a warning to the American people:

> When the people find that they can vote themselves money, that will herald the end of the republic.

Even the Father of Communism Karl Marx understood democracy's nefarious nature when he reportedly said:

> Democracy is a form of government that cannot long survive, for as soon as the people learn that they have a voice in the fiscal policies of the government, they will move to vote for themselves all the money in the treasury, and bankrupt the nation.

Unfortunately, with the help of "Obama's Army," also known as the NEA-WEAC-AFT-SEIU-AFL-CIO-AFSCME-UAW-ILWU-IWW-CPUSA-SPUSA, et al, and the Democratic Party, they have found the peoples' money. If you think what is happening in Europe can't happen here, you are mistaken. When Teamsters President Jimmy Hoffa spoke before a Democratic union crowd in Detroit, Michigan, in 2011, he used union mobocratic language and threats "Greek democracy style." Here's what he said:

> We got to keep an eye on the battle that we face: The war on workers. And you see it everywhere; it is the Tea Party. And you know, there is only one way to beat and win that war. The one thing about working people is we like a good fight. And you know what? They've got a war, they got a war with us and there's only going to be one winner. It's going to be the workers of Michigan,

and America. We're going to win that war... President Obama, this is your army. We are ready to march. Let's take these sons of bitches out and give America back to an America where we belong.

After Hoffa declared war on hardworking America citizens, President Obama walked to the podium embracing not only Hoffa's body but also his ideas! Wake up America! They want to "take us out!" We are in a cultural and political war to destroy our Republic under God!

It is a shame to see that during the "Recall Walker is Hitler" movement WEAC has no room for freedom of speech or thought. WEAC and their cohorts harass, denigrate, and intimidate in Saul Alinsky style any teacher or citizen brave enough to defend Governor Walker and challenge their mobocratic ways. I wonder if this public school teacher will ever be welcomed into a public school classroom again after this book is published. Kristi Lacroix, a teacher in the Kenosha School District who had the courage to exercise her First Amendment right to free speech in an ad opposing the recall effort against Wisconsin Governor Scott Walker, is one such sad example of public union slander. Lacroix states, according to a report by Education Action Group:

> Going through and deleting my daily amount of hate mail that is sent to my work email. I have now been assured, by one of the emails (all of which I forward to my Principal) that there is an online movement called "Fire Kristi" where they are going to email, post, and

talk to everyone (telling) millions of stories to ruin my reputation, career, and life.

Kristi Lacroix and any teachers like her do not defy WEAC for the fun of it. They do so after years and years of seeing union power destroy their ability to teach above Democratic Party politics. It is troubling to the citizens of Wisconsin when a public school teacher has the boldness to support Governor Walker's reforms and then is harassed by union thugs and Democratic operatives. Here's an example of one of many ugly emails sent to Lacroix:

> On Facebook there are lots of people willing to join the "Fire Kristi" movement. You are alone in a wilderness. Your financial help from the likes of the Koch brothers will dry up once your liabilities outweigh your assets, which will be very soon. Your best bet is to start a job search soon. Enjoy your isolation.

Isolation and intimidation are but a few of the fear factors thrown at teachers like Lacroix who dare to challenge the politically correct Democratic and union powers that be.

Kyle Olson, CEO of Education Action Group and author of *Indoctrination: How "Useful Idiots" Are Using Our Schools to Subvert America's Exceptionalism*, sums up with spot-on clarity public sector union harassment when teachers like Lacroix step out of line. He writes:

> If Big Labor is known for anything, it's lowering itself, it's lowering itself to whatever disgusting level is necessary to get what it wants. In the world of collective

bargaining and group think, the end always justified the means, regardless of how nasty the tactics might be. We find it interesting that union members want to get Lacroix fired, yet scream bloody murder when anyone mentions the possibility of firing incompetent teachers. Union leaders and radical union teachers are all about self-preservation. They are not about quality education or the best interests of students. We believe the people of Wisconsin are starting to figure that out, due largely to outrageous behavior like the constant harassment of a teacher who dares to disagree with the almighty WEAC."

When I saw Kristi Lacroix's defense of Governor Walker, I was not only taken back to my Fox & Friends defense of Governor Walker, but to my two decades-plus of wonderful times of teaching my students a love of America's exceptionalism and this great constitutional Republic under God. Unfortunately, many other thoughts came to my mind about the numerous times I was intimidated by the powers-that-be to not waver off the politically correct path. From being pro-life to admiring Ronald Reagan to teaching on the Christian heritage of America, many times I was reprimanded for crossing the line and speaking the truth. And that was in a relatively conservative part of Wisconsin. Imagine what it must be like teaching in Milwaukee or Madison when the mobsters attack teachers brave enough to teach the truth. They don't last long on the job.

They need our prayers and a good constitutional, non-ACLU lawyer!

When you read Kristi Lacroix's thoughts on her Facebook page, your heart can truly empathize with her.

She writes:

> I have sat by for my 14 years and have been saddened by the amount of non-learning that is allowed to take place in our school. The unions are destroying public education and it makes me sick that these are the people who represent the teachers who are wonderful, do a good job, and are a vital part of children's lives. I just don't fit in the education system. I would like to actively search for a new job where I can still work with kids and not have to work for public education. I just want a classroom, students, and to be left alone to teach.

I cannot say it any better than Kyle Olson who writes:

> You're absolutely right, Ms. Lacroix. You do not fit into a public education system that in many cities has become little more than a financial grab bag for multi-million-dollar teachers' unions. You do not fit into a system that protects incompetent teachers and fails to reward excellent ones.

> But you do sound like a dedicated educator who cares about kids. That means you would probably fit quite nicely into a charter or private school. And perhaps someday, when taxpayers reclaim their schools from the self-serving unions, you can go back and work in public schools that are focused solely on the single issue that should concern them—student learning.

It must be noted that, like Kristi, there are many dedicated public school teachers in Wisconsin. I know. I worked with them in many school districts (I was a substitute teacher for a year) and learned from them at the many conferences I attended throughout my career. These dedicated teachers did not let Democratic and union political intimidation and indoctrination get the best of them. But unfortunately, I have also known a number of teachers who were driven by Democratic and union politics to slant their curriculum, bias their teaching, and blind their eyes to the one-sidedness of their ways. It is sad to say that I saw this one-sidedness in droves during the 2011 "Walker is Hitler" rallies in Madison, Wisconsin.

Remember my chapter on the NEA and their top lawyer saying they were about money, power, and not the kids? Well, before Governor Walker came along, public school unions like the MTEA (Milwaukee Teachers Education Association) were suing the Milwaukee school district for male discrimination for taking away their "right" to have Viagra in their health insurance package. No wonder they have a bone to pick with the Governor Walker! He understands how bizarre and arrogant the teachers' unions and mobocrats have gotten with our money, and thanks to him and our Republican representatives, that kind of nonsense has stopped in Wisconsin.

Let's pray that Wisconsin citizens stop the Democrats at their mobocratic "Walker is Hitler Recall" attempt. Let's hope that reasoned citizens will once again vote within "a republican form of government," expressing their voice that the minority mob will not prevail!

As I travel America giving my Tea Party and Republic-under-God speeches, I speak with many hardworking, middle-class Americans like Samuel "Joe the Plumber" Wurzelbacher, Wisconsin senators Ron Johnson, Frank Lasee, and Pam Galloway, representatives Michelle Litjens, Andre Jacque, and Jim Steineke, Lieutenant Governor Rebecca Kleefisch, and Julaine Appling of Wisconsin Family Counsel. I am impressed with their integrity, work ethic, and understanding of our Founders' vision for our republic and their dedication to fight for limited constitutional republicanism.

The same mobocratic big-government battle that is being waged at the state level in Madison, Wisconsin, is being fought at the federal level in Washington, D.C. Wisconsin conservative warriors like my high school friend Congressman Reid Ribble left his very successful business due to his concern over the explosion of the federal government and its superfluous spending and tyrannical taxing. Reid, along with the majority of Republicans in the House of Representatives, is fighting daily for republican virtue, fiscal responsibility, and traditional values.

Another Wisconsin conservative warrior is Congressman Paul Ryan who calls for recapturing the "American Idea." Ryan was named Conservative of the Year by Human Events magazine. During an interview with its editor-at-large Jason Mattera, he articulated his Founding Fathers' vision:

[The election] is a referendum on the American idea, not on Barack Obama and his handling of the economy... It is, do you want to reclaim the founding principles that made us exceptional and great, an opportunity society with a circumscribed safety net? Or do you want the cradle-to-grave welfare state? It's really a choice of two futures... We owe it to the country to let them choose what kind of country they want to be and what kind of people they want to be... the debt crisis can't be stressed enough. To put in perspective just how much of an anvil this Administration's policies are to the economy, Obama has tacked on more to the national debt than the first 41 presidents combined (George Washington to George Bush), and he's done so in a mere 32 months.

Wisconsin Congressman Paul Ryan concludes his interview by saying:

The next two years will make it or break it: whether we go back to our limited government [and] economic freedom or a European social democracy.

Freedom or European social democracy! That is what this cultural and political war to destroy our Republic under God is all about.

What cultural and political philosophy will we leave our children and our children's children?

Will freedom and constitutional republicanism continue in America or will European social democracy and its variant offshoots of big-government statism, socialism, cultural Marxism, and secular progressivism prevail in the end? Will we heed the warnings of our Founders or will we go the way of nations that have come and gone?

America is dying because America's children are not being taught VERITAS, or the truth, in our classrooms. When America's culture gives credence to the Whoopi Goldbergs, Sean Penns, Susan Sarandons, and Matt Damons of the world who think communism is a great concept on paper as they cross their fingers hoping that the "right" leader comes along to implement it properly, you know we are on a slippery slope to socialism. When Americans ignored all the warnings of Barack Obama's socialist ties and ways, you know our Republic under God is on the precipice of survival. When the favorite symbol in the "Walker is Hitler" and Occupy rallies is the socialist Days of Rage clenched fist, you know it is becoming more and more difficult to keep our republic in peace. When our President's advisors are card-carrying communists like Van Jones, or admirers of Mao Zedong like Anita Dunn, or red-letter Marxists like Jim Wallis, you know our days of trusting in God are diminishing as the people turn to government as their God and Savior.

Back in my college days in Arizona, I once bagged Sandra Day O'Connor's groceries at the Safeway grocery store where I worked. Ironically, it was the same store where Nancy Reagan's parents used to shop. When President Reagan appointed Judge O'Connor to be the first woman on the Supreme Court, I was blessed to congratulate her on her historic appointment in the Safeway parking lot.

That was thirty-one years ago and since then we have taken a hard-Left turn for the worse as we follow the path of European socialism. As bleak and dismal as it may seem, there is hope!

We are Americans. Freedom is wired in our DNA. Our veins pump with the blood of liberty, and our hearts are willing to fight tyranny in its many manifestations.

We must match our hearts with our minds!

Anti-republicanism can be stopped through knowledge and education on the wonderful miraculous origin of our great constitutional Republic under God!

Thirty-one years later as I conclude writing my book on mobocracy, retired Supreme Court Justice Sandra Day O'Connor spoke in late December 2011 to a number of high school students at the Ronald Reagan Presidential Library in Simi Valley, California. She spoke on how disturbed she is over the "lack of public knowledge" Americans have about American history, civics, and constitutional republicanism. In 2006, Justice O'Connor launched iCivics, an online program aimed at educating middle-school students on our republican form of government. Thanks to technology, more and more alternative educational programs, schools, and organizations are available as more and more citizens are frustrated with the direction of politically correct, left-wing indoctrination that is being manifested in America's public schools and institutions.

As we wind down our discourse on mobocracy in America, I reflect on the Adams family, which I do not for a moment think were creepy, kooky, or spooky. John Adams has been called the "voice of the Declaration of Independence." He was America's first vice president and second president. He was a great Founding Father who passionately hated slavery of any kind. From African slavery to the slavery of socialism, Adams dedicated his whole life to speaking out against the stealing or coveting of property as we see expressed today by big-government socialism. In 1787, John Adams wrote the following in his book, *A Defense of the Constitutions of Government of the United States of America*:

> The moment the idea is admitted into society that property is not as sacred as the laws of God, and that there is not a force of law and public justice to protect it, anarchy and tyranny commence. If "Thou shalt not covet" and "Thou shalt not steal" were not commandments of Heaven, they must be made inviolable precepts in every society before it can be civilized or made free.

John Adams' son, John Quincy, was equally a champion of life and liberty, and in his 1839 discourse, *The Jubilee of the Constitution*, he wrote this:

> Fellow-citizens, the ark of your covenant is the Declaration of Independence. Your Mount Ebal is the confederacy of separate state sovereignties, and your Mount Gerizim is the Constitution of the United States. In that scene of tremendous and awful solemnity, narrated in the Holy Scriptures, there is not a curse pronounced against the people, upon Mount Ebal, not a blessing promised them upon Mount Gerizim, which your posterity may not suffer or enjoy, from your and their adherence to, or departure from, the principles of the Declaration of

Independence, practically interwoven in the Constitution of the United States. Lay up these principles, then, in your hearts, and in your souls—bind them for signs upon your hands, that they may be as frontlets between your eyes—teach them to your children, speaking of them when sitting in your houses, when walking by the way, when lying down and when rising up—write them upon the doorplates of your houses, and upon your gates—cling to them as to the issues of life—adhere to them as to the cords of your eternal salvation. So may your children's children at the next return of this day of jubilee, after a full century of experience under your national Constitution, celebrate it again in the full enjoyment of all the blessings recognized by you in the commemoration of this day, and of all the blessings promised to the children of Israel upon Mount Gerizim, as the reward of obedience to the law of God.

Notice how both Adams' invoke the Judeo-Christian law of God and how our sixth president, John Quincy, with profound biblical symbolism, talks of laying the principles of the Constitution in our hearts and our children's hearts and souls 24/7/365.

Americans are waking up, as they have grown tired of succumbing to the NEA, union mobsters, the social Democratic Party, and to secular progressive and socialistic machinations, which with socialist clenched fist held high, cry out in defiance of our republican form of government:

"This is what democracy looks like!"

"A republic, if you can keep it." Benjamin Franklin's departing words at the 1787 Constitutional Convention echo down the corridors of American history. Franklin's words beckon us to go beyond "sunshine Patriotism." The Greek word Nike means victory. Fellow Americans, for us to be victorious we must get off the couch, put on our running shoes, and "Just do it." Our republic calls out to all of us who love life, liberty, and limited government under God. It is time to organize, mobilize, and educate across our great land in 2012 and beyond to STOP Obama's army of cultural and political big-government mobocrats before it is too late.

In Governor Walker's 2011 inaugural address he called for the reestablishment of frugality, virtue and fundamental republican principles. In like manner President George Washington taught us about the "sacred fire of liberty" when he said this in his 1789 inaugural address:

> Since we ought to be no less persuaded that the propitious smiles of Heaven can never be expected on a nation that disregards the eternal rules of order and right which Heaven itself has ordained; and since the preservation of the sacred fire of liberty and the destiny of the republican model of government are justly considered, perhaps, as deeply, as finally, staked on the experiment entrusted to the hands of the American people.

Thank you, President Dwight Eisenhower, for fighting National Socialism in the '40s and for fighting International Socialism in the '50s. Thank you for setting the record straight with fixing

America's pledge of allegiance that reflects our constitutional republican form of government under God.

We need to elect and keep in office in Washington, D.C.—in the White House, the Senate, and the House of Representatives, and in Madison—the Governor's house, the Senate, and the Assembly, authentic Republicans who truly believe in and abide by our constitutional Republic under God.

> I pledge allegiance to the flag of the United States of America, and to the republic for which it stands, one nation under God, indivisible, with liberty and justice for all.

This book is written "for the Republic for which it stands, one nation under God." My hope and my prayer is that you will dedicate your life, your fortunes, and your sacred honor to God, family, and to our republic so we can keep it for our children and their children and their children's children and many more...

Semper Fi to our Republic under God!

Jake Jacobs in Madison, the State Capital, with a Walker supporter

Recommended Education Sources

The Declaration of Independence

The Constitution

The Federalist Papers

The Anti-Federalist Papers

ConservativeDailyNews.com

Religion and The Founding of The American Republic: Library of Congress — http://www.loc.gov/exhibits/religion/

National Center for Constitutional Studies — http://nccs.net/

Freedom Project Education — http://fpeusa.org/(The BEST Online K-12 Classical Constitutional Republic Education in America!)

Wisconsin Family Council — http://www.wifamilyaction.org/wifamilycouncil

Young American Foundation — http://www.yaf.org/

The Heritage Foundation — http://www.heritage.org/

Frontpage Mag.com — http://frontpagemag.com/

Providence Forum — http://www.providenceforum.org/

Wallbuilders — http://www.wallbuilders.com/

Hillsdale College

Liberty University

Patrick Henry College

About the Author

Dr. Jacobs is president and founder of the Politically Incorrect Institute and has degrees in American History and Biblical and Judeo-Christian Studies. He has spent more than 25 years in the public school system teaching his passion for our Constitutional Republic under God, all the while stressing historical correctness, in the face of politically correct intimidation by the academic establishment.

Dr. Jacobs has publicly defended Wisconsin Governor Scott Walker on Fox & Friends and is a regular guest on Conservative Radio and at Tea Party events and churches. He is a dynamic and energized speaker, writer, and historian who will not only get your audience's attention, but move them to action!

To schedule Dr. Jacobs for your event, contact him at www.jjusa.org.

Dr. Jake Jacobs with Wisconsin Governor Scott Walker